Teach

Students to Write

Argument

Essays That Define

Comparison/Contrast Essays

Personal Narratives

Research Reports

▶ **Fictional Narratives**

Peter Smagorinsky

Larry R. Johannessen

Elizabeth A. Kahn

Thomas M. McCann

HEINEMANN

Portsmouth, NH

The Dynamics of Writing Instruction series

Heinemann
361 Hanover Street
Portsmouth, NH 03801–3912
www.heinemann.com

Offices and agents throughout the world

© 2012 by Peter Smagorinsky, Elizabeth A. Kahn, and Thomas M. McCann

All rights reserved. No part of this book may be reproduced in any form
or by any electronic or mechanical means, including information storage
and retrieval systems, without permission in writing from the publisher,
except by a reviewer, who may quote brief passages in a review.

"Dedicated to Teachers" is a trademark of Greenwood Publishing Group, Inc.

The authors and publisher wish to thank those who have generously
given permission to reprint borrowed material:

Excerpts from "Joe Magarac, Pittsburgh Steel Man" in *Tall Tale America:
A Legendary History of Our Humorous Heroes* by Walter Blair. Copyright ©
1987 by Walter Blair. Illustrations copyright © 1987 by John Sandford.
Published by the University of Chicago Press, Chicago, IL 60637. Re-
printed by permission of the publisher. All rights reserved.

Library of Congress Cataloging-in-Publication Data
Smagorinsky, Peter.
   Teaching students to write fictional narratives / Peter Smagorinsky ... [et al.].
       p. cm. — (The dynamics of teaching writing series)
   Includes bibliographical references.
   ISBN-13: 978-0-325-03399-0
   ISBN-10: 0-325-03399-4
   1. Language arts (Secondary). 2. English language—Composition and
exercises—Study and teaching (Secondary). 3. Storytelling. I. Title.
LB1576.S584 2012
428.0071'2—dc23   2011034010

Editor: Anita Gildea *and* Lisa Luedeke
Development editor: Alan Huisman
Production: Vicki Kasabian
Cover design: Monica Ann Crigler
Typesetter: Valerie Levy / Drawing Board Studios
Manufacturing: Steve Bernier

Printed in the United States of America on acid-free paper

15 14 13 12 PAH 2 3 4 5

CONTENTS

Preface

Despite all the attention that writing instruction received during the last decades of the twentieth century, the teaching of writing in middle and high schools remains, at best, uneven. National Writing Project sites have conducted countless summer institutes, and new books about teaching writing appear routinely in publishers' catalogues. Yet assessments continue to find that students' writing is less accomplished than teachers might hope. Undoubtedly, the assessments themselves are not what they ought to be (Hillocks 2002). But even those with relatively good reputations, such as the National Assessment of Educational Progress, find that students in the United States are not writing as well as many people expect them to. What's going on here? And will yet another book about teaching writing make a difference?

We have written this series of small books in the hope that they will provide alternatives for teachers who are dissatisfied with teaching five-paragraph themes, traditional grammar lessons, and other form-driven writing approaches. This book employs what we call *structured process*, an approach developed by George Hillocks during his years as a middle school English teacher in Euclid, Ohio, during the 1960s. Hillocks and his students have researched this method and found it highly effective (Hillocks, Kahn, and Johannessen 1983; Smith 1989; Smagorinsky 1991; Lee 1993). In a comprehensive research review, Hillocks (1986) found that over a twenty-year period, structured process writing instruction provided greater gains for student writers than did any other method of teaching writing.

We have also spent a collective 120-plus years using structured process instruction in our high school English classes. We do not claim to have discovered the one best way to teach writing; rather, our goal is to explain in detail a method that we all found successful in our teaching. We hope you find this book useful and that your teaching benefits from reading and using the entire series.

How to Get the Most Out of This Book and This Series

The six books in this series help middle and high school teachers teach writing using a structured process approach, a method based on sound theory and research. Each book follows a similar format, focusing on a different type of writing: fictional narrative (the focus of this volume), personal narrative, essays that define, comparison/contrast essays, argument, and research reports. Although there are some general writing processes that apply to all types of writing, different kinds of writing require unique strategies. Therefore, the instructional activities in each book are tailored to that specific kind of writing.

The books show you how to design and orchestrate activities within an interactive and collaborative environment in which your students themselves experiment with ideas, debate these ideas with their peers, decide what and how to write, determine how to assess the quality of their writing, and discuss their work as a group. They include classroom-tested activities, detailed lesson sequences, and supporting handouts. The instruction is detailed enough to use as a daily lesson plan but general enough that you can modify it to accommodate your own curriculum and the specific needs of your students.

Most writing instruction emphasizes form. With a structured process approach, students first learn the thinking processes and strategies at the heart of a specific kind of writing, then consider form. This approach also recognizes that students write best when they want to communicate something that matters to them. The books show you how to introduce issues, dilemmas, and scenarios that capture students' interest and invoke the critical and creative thinking necessary to write powerfully and effectively. Samples of student writing are included; they illustrate students' learning and can also be used as instructional material for students to critique.

You may incorporate these books into a multiyear English language arts program, perhaps starting with personal narratives and fictional narratives in the earlier grades and moving to arguments, comparison/contrast essays, essays that define, and research reports in later grades. Alternatively, all six books in the series could constitute a yearlong writing course. Another option is to repeat modified sequences from one book at sequential grade levels, so students deal with that particular form at increasing degrees of complexity.

Although many of the activities and teaching strategies in these books can be used in isolation, they are most effective when included within a sequence of instruction in which students participate in increasingly challenging activities designed to help them become independent writers.

What's in This Book

A brief introduction explains what we mean by *fictional narrative* and also why we believe it's important to teach students to do this kind of writing (as well as the thinking related to it). Chapters 1 through 4 show you *how* to teach students to write fictional narratives using structured process instruction; in them we describe classroom teaching strategies, provide a sequence of activities and handouts, and show examples of student work. Chapter 5 explains the structured process approach to teaching writing and its two main tenets, *environmental teaching* and *inquiry instruction*. This will help you understand why we designed the instruction modeled in this book the way we did; it will also help you design your own units of instruction in the future.

Why Teach Students to Write Fictional Narratives?

The high school common core standards emphasize that students will develop proficiency in writing both arguments and narratives. The standard for narrative writing states: "Write narratives to develop real or imagined experiences or events using effective technique, well-chosen details, and well-structured event sequences." Similarly, the College Readiness Standards offered by the College Board emphasize unity, organization, and coherence as key features of strong writing.

While it is encouraging to see core standards that affirm the importance of learning to write well, students in middle school and high school are seldom asked to produce extended writing of any sort (Applebee and Langer 2009). Even more rare are opportunities to write narratives, the implication being that teachers and administrators don't think narrative writing prepares learners for college and future careers or will help them do well on state assessments and other standardized tests.

This apparent disregard for the value of having students write narratives is curious given that the bulk of students' experience with literature in middle school and high school involves fiction. It appears teachers celebrate the fiction writing of accomplished authors but steer students away from writing their own fiction.

The real question is not whether to ask students to write arguments or narratives but how to teach students to write a variety of texts, including fictional narratives. It is of course true that the procedures required in writing one genre help students plan, draft, and refine their efforts in another. Certainly the attention to detail and specificity fictional narratives require help a writer compose an essay that defines or persuades.

We offer three lines of thought if you need to justify teaching your students to write fictional narratives. First—and perhaps most pragmatic when ramping up test scores is of concern—the skills that students learn in writing narratives apply to other writing. This is not to say that all writing processes are interchangeable: any writing situation presents particular needs and challenges. But the goal of providing enough detail while at the same time remaining concise and coherent also applies when one is supplying illustrative and contrasting examples to support an extended definition. Vignettes and scenarios can also be used as examples to support claims in an argument. When developing a comparison/contrast piece, one might tell two stories that seem similar on the surface but have notable distinctions on closer examination.

Bruner (1991) reminds us that narratives help thinkers understand the world around them. Organizing a sequence of events into a discernible pattern can help someone recall what has happened and understand its significance. In developing a fictional narrative, a writer tries to understand human motivation and emotion—why characters do the things they do and act on the emotions they feel. A fictional narrative can also represent how fellow human beings should behave and how the world should function. Writing fiction is a tool for thinking, for making sense of what a writer experiences.

Writing fictional narratives also supports students' understanding of what they read. When student writers produce texts that parallel and imitate the fiction they read, they can intuit a new but related text more easily and are better prepared to interpret a storyteller's generalizations and evaluate her or his craft.

In his influential book on teaching narrative writing, Hillocks (2006) provides detailed guidance on how to help students write narratives. He notes that writing fiction involves *invention* and *organization*. Perhaps the invention part gives you pause. How do you teach students to invent the substance of a fictional narrative? Simply put, learning to invent the substance of a story is socially mediated, as is all manner of learning. Through structured inquiry, students learn about various fiction genres and find ways to invent stories.

The following chapters illustrate a structured process approach for teaching students to write fictional narratives. Chapter 1 offers lessons that help students write simple narratives. Chapter 2 provides structures that encourage students to write collaboratively and develop a means-end composing strategy. Chapters 3 and 4 examine more elaborate and individual expressions, including creating suspense and relying on evocative visual images to prompt characters, settings, and situations. The writing students produce themselves introduces them to structures and themes they will encounter in their study of literature. Chapter 5 explains the structured process approach in a bit more detail.

The activities in each chapter are problem-based. Students, in groups, explore possible solutions to a specific, concrete, familiar problem. There is a specific audience to address, a central purpose for writing, a body of information to be examined, and a framework for completing the analysis. Students can solve the problem in a variety of ways given their overall purpose and specified constraints. They are not telling their stories for the sake of storytelling but rather to accomplish a goal. Ideally, while thinking and talking with their peers, they develop procedures they can use independently in other situations, with other content.

By deliberately working through several stages on the way to completing an immediate product, students have an opportunity to tell a story that both matters to them and conveys experiences vividly to others. They address a particular problem using specific problem-solving strategies and rehearse their stories with other students before they put them on paper. Creating the narrative helps them understand their own experiences and the experiences they encounter in the fiction they study.

Teaching Students to Write Short Fictional Narratives

Narratives take a variety of forms, from simple to complex. Sometimes the most admired are those that defy traditional conventions. While one can certainly generalize about the composing process for writing narratives, each type of narrative has distinct characteristics. Understanding the demands of the various forms lets you design lessons that help students define the forms and generate their own stories. Each writing situation presents its own challenges and requires that you analyze what the task demands: What must the writer know? What must the writer be able to do?

Lessons on how to write fables, which require a relatively simple story structure, are appropriate for both younger and more mature writers. Students also explore *theme*, which the fable makes obvious through the expression of a *moral* (you might also discuss how the development pattern allows one to infer a theme). In addition, students investigate examples of *symbol*, *personification*, and *metaphor*.

The tall tale exposes students to a folk narrative tradition that relies on exaggeration to signal readers that the tale is not intended to be believed. Students have fun composing their own tall tales, and the contrast between expressed meaning and intended meaning introduces them to *irony*. The tall tale characters selected and the specific exaggerations in their treatment reflect the values admired by the culture of which the author is a part, another aspect of literary study.

Task Analysis: Writing Fables

By the end of a series of lessons on how to write fables, you expect your students to be able to:

1. Identify the characteristics of a fable.

2. Recognize the use of personification.

3. Recognize and interpret various animal species as symbols of human shortcomings.

4. Evaluate the moral of a fable by comparing it with their own life experiences.

5. Describe the setting.

6. Sequence events logically.

7. Write dialogue using the correct conventions (e.g., punctuation, paragraphing, dialogue tags).

8. Write a fable.

Stage 1. Defining the Conventions

Examine fables written by Aesop, Jean de la Fontaine, Italo Calvino, Rafael Pombo, Arnold Lobel, or James Thurber (many examples are available online; see Bartleby.com), as well as examples of fables written by students in your classes in previous years, whose vocabulary and syntax will be similar to that of your current students. Rather than introducing the term *fable* and giving students a list of characteristics, have students examine a number of fables, identify what the stories have in common, and note how the better stories differ from the less appealing ones.

EPISODE 1.1. Tell students they are going to read a group of very short stories that all have a number of characteristics in common. Read Aesop's "Belling the Cat" aloud (don't identify the genre), revealing your inner thinking as you go along: *What kind of mice would have a council? Isn't it strange that mice would meet in council and discuss a problem? Does the author expect me to believe that mice can really talk? What is a tyrant?*

Discuss the *moral* by asking volunteers to rephrase the message expressed at the end of the story. Ask students whether they've ever known anyone who acted the way the characters in the story act. What happened to him or her? What do they think about this type of person? Why?

Next, distribute copies of three more stories (see Figures 1–1, 1–2, and 1–3) and ask student volunteers to read them aloud. Have students retell each one and explain and evaluate the moral.

Figure 1–1. An Angry Crow

Once upon a time a young and independent crow descended to a country road just as three other crows were cleaning the last bit of flesh from a squirrel that had been struck by a car. The young crow confronted the others: "You have cleaned every bit of meat from that animal. Why couldn't you have saved a bit for me?" The oldest of the crows responded, "You have to be quick about these things. You never know when another meal will be available. Stay with us and perhaps we can share the next meal together." Angry about the perceived slight, the young crow flew off without responding. He hoped to find a means of tricking the other crows out of a meal so that they would know how it felt to be left out.

So the young crow fashioned a plan to trick the others. He worked for the rest of the afternoon gathering mud and bits of tree moss and using them to shape a figure along the side of the road that he thought looked like the carcass of a squirrel. By the time he had finished, he was tired and famished. Then the other crows happened along and asked, "Where have you been? We have just eaten the most enormous meal of raccoon and field mouse. You should have been with us!" The young crow could only respond by kicking the figure that he had spent hours constructing.

Sometimes revenge harms only the avenger.

Figure 1–2. The Busy Hippopotamus

After working first as a dishwasher, then a server, and then a cook at a restaurant, a hippopotamus was elevated to the position of assistant manager. Once installed in this lofty position, the hippopotamus could not help but look at the other staff critically. She recognized that she could do their jobs better than they were doing the jobs themselves. She began taking reservations, which was normally the penguin's responsibility. She rushed outside to park cars for the hyena valets. She then assumed the responsibility of the walrus, who waited tables. After taking orders, she dashed behind the fountain to prepare sodas and hustled to the kitchen to push the gorilla from the stove to prepare the meal in her own way. After delivering the meals, she leaped to the stage and replaced the flamingo in the floorshow.

After fielding the complaints of the staff, the restaurant owner confronted the aggressive hippopotamus: "Why are you trying to do everyone else's job? In this way you have managed to insult everyone, and you have neglected your own responsibilities."

"I helped out, because I knew that I could do the work better."

"You might be better than any one person," said the owner, "but in trying to do everyone's job, you make the whole restaurant less."

Pride in your ability does not give you the right to diminish the contributions of others.

EPISODE 1.2. Organize students into groups of three. Give the groups fifteen minutes to list and discuss at least *three* things the stories have in common: i.e., how are the three stories similar? Then have a representative from each group share the group's observations with the whole class. Record these observations on the board and ask students to list them in their notebooks. Here are some possible observations:

All the stories include animal characters.

The animals act like people. (You might ask students how they know.)

> **Figure 1–3.** The Bear and the Sloth
>
> Bear and Sloth strolled along and entered a woods together in search of nuts and insect nests. But Sloth suddenly hesitated. "I know these woods," Sloth said. "Last year hunters came and took away several of my friends. I dare not step farther. I'll rest here."
>
> "My dear friend Sloth," said Bear, "you are the laziest and most cowardly one I know. I have no fear of walking in any woods. Look at the size of me, my remarkable girth, my knifelike claws, my menacing teeth. No hunter will dare to challenge me."
>
> "All the same," said Sloth, "I prefer to wait for you here, even if I must go hungry for now."
>
> Bear entered the woods. A short time later, Sloth heard the familiar sound of the reports from two rifles. His friend Bear did not return.
>
> *Confidence in your ability is no reason to ignore real danger.*

The animals talk (which means there is dialogue).

There is a message (moral, lesson) at the end.

The message is about humans, not animals.

The stories are short—less than one page long.

Something bad happens to one of the characters.

Seeing how something bad happens to the character, you learn not to be like that character.

Through their small- and large-group discussions, students identify the basic elements of a fable. When the students write their own original fables, the features they have identified become the criteria for determining, in self or peer reviews, whether they have written the fable successfully.

EPISODE 1.3. Ask the three-member groups to examine the fable examples again and rank them from best to worst. Each group should try to reach a consensus (disagreement is okay) and be prepared to explain their rankings to the rest of the class. In their discussions the students refine their standards for judging the quality not only of the fables they read but also of the ones they write.

Next, have a representative from each group report the group's rankings to the class. Ask the whole class to agree on a set of characteristics for distinguishing good stories from less appealing stories. Characteristics may include:

> The story was easy to follow (there was clear sequence of events).
>
> I could picture what was going on (use of descriptive details, effective use of dialogue).
>
> I liked the characters.
>
> I agreed with the message of the story.

As the students discuss their observations, paraphrase and elaborate as necessary. Record the students' comments on the board (and ask students to add these ideas to their notes) as the basis for distinguishing between a high-quality fable and a mediocre one.

EPISODE 1.4.   Give this writing assignment:

> I want each of you to write a story in which animals act like humans. One way they act like humans is by talking. Something bad happens to one of the characters, from which the reader learns a lesson: for example, don't be greedy; don't be conceited; don't be mean. In other words, the message criticizes something unpleasant you have observed in other human beings. Refer to your notes for the specific criteria, determined in our class discussions, that will be used to evaluate your work.

Stage 2. Composing Stories

EPISODE 2.1.   Ask the students, working independently, to make a brief list of four or five things other persons do that really bother them (for example, I don't like people who don't tell the truth; I don't like people who talk loudly on their cell phones in restaurants; I don't like people who throw trash out of their car windows). After a few moments, have everyone share ideas as you list them on the board. After all the ideas have been listed, ask students to suggest particular animals that might be associated with a particular problem: What kind of animal would be a liar? What kind of animal would talk loudly on a cell phone? What kind of animal would throw trash out of a car window? Below are some examples of negative traits and animals that might be associated with them:

Negative Trait	Animal
Lying	Snake
Smoking	Lizard
Talking behind a friend's back	Fox
Being lazy	Sloth
Being greedy	Pig
Complaining	Blue jay
Manipulating	Coyote
Bullying	Shark

As students match an animal with a particular trait, ask them to explain why someone would associate this animal with this problem. Why would someone think a snake is a liar, for example, or a lizard is a smoker? As the students explain their reasoning, they will begin to generate a story. For example, a student may say, "I think a blue jay would be complaining all the time because blue jays make a lot of noise. And they have these real loud cries, like they're angry about something."

EPISODE 2.2.   After the students have discussed many possible associations of particular animals with particular negative traits, ask them to draft a story: What is a problem that you dislike in other persons? What kind of animal would act like this? What could happen to the animal so that the animal would learn that there is a problem?

Before they begin, have them reiterate the characteristics of the fable and recount the features that distinguish a good story. Also model converting indirect quotations to direct quotations, supplying dialogue tags, beginning new paragraphs to mark the change in speaker, and capitalizing proper names. You might also provide a vignette and ask students to provide appropriate dialogue. (See Hillocks 2006 for more on teaching students the conventions of dialogue.)

Stage 3. Reviewing and Refining Fables

When students have completed their drafts, offer them options for refining them. For example, you might have a conference in which you make comments and ask questions related to the evaluation criteria the students developed earlier. Or students can share their writing with each other, again referring to the original criteria and also relying on their intuitive sense of what "flowed" or resonated with them. After students have made their final revisions, collect all the fables and assemble them into a class anthology, either in print or online. Figures 1–4 and 1–5 are examples of student fables.

Figure 1–4. "The Flamingo," by Tyler Sidoryk

Deep in a jungle, by a pool of water, a group of flamingos danced and ate happily. One of the flamingos emerged from the bushes. "Look at my beautiful colors! They must be shining!" Everyone agreed that his feathers were the color of a pink sunset, and he had the most colorful body of all.

Moray, the competitive one, who was used to being the best, was jealous. Really jealous. He secretly left the group and went in search of the source of color. It wasn't long before he stumbled on a small pond. This pond was full of colorful shrimp. "This must be where he got his beauty. I'll eat so much shrimp that no one will ever be as colorful as me!" he thought, and gulped down shrimp for hours, dozens at a time. He stared at himself for hours in amazement before hurrying back to the group. "Look, everybody! Look! Look! Look!" His whole body was a fiery red like a bonfire. Everyone ohhhhed and ahhhhed with interest.

They were all happy and joyful until a small bird came chirping in over the trees. "Hunters!" he screeched. "Hunters are coming!" There was a moment of hesitation; then the birds all squawked and yelled, flying into trees, running out of the clearing. Moray ate so much shrimp that he couldn't run so he hid behind the nearest bush and waited. It wasn't long before he

Figure 1–4. "The Flamingo," by Tyler Sidoryk (*continued*)

realized his colors were so exuberant that they could be seen through the bush! The first bullet whizzed past his neck; the second missed him by an inch. With as much energy as he had, he flew to one of the low branches, where he stayed and was safe.

Don't be carelessly proud, for it can be your undoing.

Figure 1–5. "The Bossy Kangaroo," by Carly Laurx

A privileged Kangaroo lived in a tidy home, tended by her many servants. The trees surrounding her home bent to give her an elegant paradise. Every day she ordered around her servants. You might say they were extremely fortunate to be working in such a nice household, but they were indeed quite terrified of their master—except for one, the Owl. This Owl served as a waiter in her grand dining room. Every day the bossy Kangaroo ordered him about doing extremely hard jobs that weren't even his!

Day after day he worked and worked and worked. Finally he had had enough. Soon he was standing above his master and fanning her "sweltering" body. "*Faster!*" she screeched. "Are you out of your mind? My body is aching with pains, and you fan me slow and steady? *Ugghhh*!!!" She then lowered herself with a soft and satisfied sigh as the owl batted the fan madly.

"Umm, master," the Owl began, "I do believe my fellow workers and I get quite tired of being ordered around by . . . shall we say a slightly bossy and mildly lonely person."

"What!! I am not bossy, and I, well . . ."

The Owl understood, even though he had drifted off. "You see, you are so lonely because most people do not particularly favor bossy people."

"You know, maybe you are right. I guess it is time to sweep up my act."

They both laughed hysterically at that one.

Control is not everything, when no friends are at your side.

Task Analysis: Writing Tall Tales

Use tall tales to teach students that developing characters is a key element in conveying themes. The exaggerated characters in tall tales make it relatively easy to draw inferences about the values celebrated by the author or by the author's intended audience. You not only want your students to read some tales but also expect them to write their own tales in which exaggerated characters embody some characteristics currently celebrated in American popular culture.

After completing this series of lessons, your students should be able to:

1.   Identify exaggeration in a tale.

2.   Describe the tone of a tall tale.

3.   Identify the characteristics of a tall tale.

4.   Infer the values that a tall tale character represents.

5.   Write a series of related exaggerations.

6.   Write a tall tale.

Stage 1. Understanding the Use and Appeal of Exaggeration

Although many students have been exposed to examples of tall tales, the tall tale as an oral folk tradition may be confused with fantasies and the adventures of superheroes. While all these forms may have a larger-than-life protagonist, the tall tale has unique characteristics, including a tongue-in-cheek tone that reveals the narrator's awareness that the story is ironic, as well as a structure and emphasis that together convey theme.

EPISODE 1.1.   Students need to learn to write inventive and humorous exaggerations before they can develop a full story. Spend ten minutes reading aloud several "whoppers" from American folklore (see Figure 1–6). Many examples feature contests in which participants try to tell the biggest lie. Ask students: How can we recognize that these stories are not true? What is the writer's purpose in each case?

Figure 1–6. Sample "Whoppers"

Cold Weather

I understand that it was so cold in DeKalb that the smoke froze as it came out of chimneys; and not only could you see your breath, you could grab it out of the air. Penguins moved into the abandoned house next door, and polar bears migrated south of town to find a warmer environment.

Talkers

I heard of a talking contest between two celebrated gabbers, Mike and Barb, from Parnell, Iowa. After three days of nonstop talking, both contestants fell over in exhaustion; but observers could still see Mike whispering in Barb's ear.

Crooked River

Kishwaukee Creek is so winding that when you think you have jumped over it, you land on the same side where you started. If you took a canoe trip on the creek, it would take you three days to travel the same distance you could have covered on foot in an hour.

Mosquitoes

People like to complain that their home state has the biggest mosquitoes. A man from Missouri complained that two mosquitoes flew off with his prize bloodhound. On the Upper Peninsula of Michigan, the mosquitoes grow so large that the loggers use them like rip saws to fell trees. In Louisiana, the mosquitoes are trapped, cooked, and served for dinner in some of the finest restaurants.

EPISODE 1.2.   Ask students to recall situations in which someone tried to outdo someone else—by describing a remarkable occurrence, one's current troubles, or some harrowing experience—and imitate that experience. Each exaggeration should offer a striking image rather than simply state something emphatically. Point out the difference in the following examples:

No Image:	The mosquitoes near my home are so big that they are bigger than you can imagine.
Image:	The mosquitoes near my home are so big that it would only take two of them to whip any dog in town.
Image:	The mosquitoes near my home are so big that one landed at the airport, and the attendants filled it up with jet fuel before they realized it had the wrong markings.

Display the questions below and ask students to write down some exaggerations in response. Tell them they'll then read their exaggerations aloud and have a contest to see who can create the best exaggeration.

1.   How big are the mosquitoes near your home?

2.   How fast is your car?

3.   How ugly is your (or someone else's) pet?

4.   How strong is the strongest person you know?

5.   How tough is the toughest coach you know?

6.   How thin is the thinnest person you know?

7.   How much can the hungriest person you know eat?

8.   How fast is the fastest person you know?

9.   How beautiful is the most attractive person you know?

10. How tough is your (or some other) neighborhood?

After five minutes, have students read their responses aloud, discuss them, and decide which are the best based on originality, humor, imagery, and improbability. Through this activity, students develop a sense of what elements distinguish appealing exaggerations.

Stage 2. Building the Larger Structure

EPISODE 2.1. While your students will come up with individual exaggerations that are in many instances striking and humorous, they probably won't build a series of exaggerations toward some effect. Share a series of related exaggerations and note how the related hyperboles build. Then brainstorm ways to organize a series of exaggerations.

Ask your students to revisit the exaggerations they created during the previous activity, pick the one they think is best, and develop it into a series of related exaggerations. Remind the students to use concrete images to build their series of exaggerations from smallest to greatest. Also tell them to introduce the series of exaggerations within a context, like an informal contest between two speakers or a chronicle of exceptional phenomena.

EPISODE 2.2. After each student has drafted a series of related exaggerations, divide them into groups of four. Have each group member read his or her exaggerations to the rest of the group. Ask listeners to comment on the effectiveness of each exaggeration in terms of imagery and humor and evaluate the order in which the exaggerations are presented. By sharing with their peers, students will begin thinking about how to build their exaggerations to a climax and become more aware of making each exaggeration a concrete image.

Stage 3. Defining and Producing Tall Tales

EPISODE 3.1. Distribute copies of two tall tales, "The Weakest Trucker" (Figure 1–7) and "Joe Margarac" (Figure 1–8). After students have read the stories, ask them to identify the similarities. Who is the narrator of each story? How are the narrators similar? Why is this kind of narrator used? Who is the central character?

How is the story organized? What is the writer's purpose? As students identify similar features, list them on the board—for example, one narrator turning over the narration to a second narrator, a bigger-than-life central character, a humorous tone, episodes that reveal the strengths of the central character, building to a climax.

Figure 1–7. The Weakest Trucker

I was making a long run with a load of tractor parts, heading for Vernal, Utah. I had been driving for six hours, with another four hours yet to go. It was late at night, and I reached a point where the white lines on the road began to look wavy, and my eyelids grew heavy. I thought it wise to pull into a truck stop in Limon, Colorado. I pulled up a chair at a table with a bunch of other weary truck drivers. We all ordered black coffee and complained about being tired and having many miles to go to our destinations.

Another truck driver strode into the truck stop and asked if he could join us. He introduced himself.

"Judd Bolling, a simple truck-driving man. I can't stay long," he said. "I got a load of lumber that I have to get to Topeka by mornin'. I can't stay but a minute for some coffee." The waitress poured our coffees and left the carafe. Well, Judd took that carafe and drank it down in three gulps. He asked the waitress for ten cheeseburgers wrapped to take with him. "Just come down from Seward, Alaska, and it was the prettiest ride you'll ever experience."

"You mean to tell us you've been driving over 3,000 miles? How many days did it take you?"

"I left this morning. I was delayed a bit. I thought I would save some time by driving across a frozen lake in the Yukon Territory but the lake had begun to thaw. And I had a blowout just this side of Edmonton. That delayed me, too. I brought extra gas and food, so I haven't had to stop much. But my boss expects me to make my deadlines, with no excuses."

"Now that's the toughest trucking outfit I ever heard of. How could you keep working for them?"

"I'm glad to have the job. I got fired from my last outfit for being the slowest and weakest driver in the company. Well, here are my burgers. See you, fellas."

Figure 1–8. Joe Magarac

Joe made steel his own way, of course.

First he'd collect the charge—scrap iron, coke, limestone, melted pig iron or blown Bessemer steel. Others used cars to carry the charge to the furnace, and others used the charging machine to dump it into the furnace, but not Joe. He just lugged in all this stuff by the armful, and then chucked it into the door.

You know how it is outside the furnaces in one of those Pittsburgh steel mills. The air is all choked up with heat, and most people find it tolerably warm. But Joe Magarac would go and sit right in the door of the furnace, sticking his hands in now and then, to see if the heat was right or to scoop out some brew to see if the mixture was right—for all the world like a cook tasting soup. If the mixture didn't have the right proportions, he'd heave in whatever was needed—a little coke, or limestone, or whatever would make it right for the best steel.

Finally he'd say, "The mixture's right, and the heat's just right—thirty-two hundred degrees. Guess it's time to pour out."

Then he'd go down to the back of the long row of furnaces, and get in back of number seven. At a time like that, other workers would pick at the clay and sand in the vent hole very carefully and they'd take off the last thin layer with a blow torch.

Not Joe, though. Joe'd put the ladle in place—which was quite a job in itself, since the ladle was a giant bucket that would take twenty-four tons of melted steel without stretching. Then he'd put the slag catcher in place. And then, he'd take his forefinger and tap the vent hole. Then the molten steel would come pouring out in a white rush.

When the ladle was full, others had to use cranes to pick up the ladles and dump the liquid steel into the ingot molds. Not Joe, though. Joe would cup his hands, dip up the stuff, and throw it into the molds himself.

And when the stuff was cooked enough, instead of taking it over to the rolling mill, the way others did, Joe would take the stuff in his hands and squeeze it, hard and slow.

It would come rolling out between his fingers in the prettiest rails you ever laid eyes on. (Blair 1987, 240–42)

EPISODE 3.2.   Have students look again at the series of related exaggerations they have written. Ask them to identify the human attribute they have exaggerated—for example, size, strength, courage, a specific skill. Write these attributes on the board. Then ask students to write down two or three characters who might possess each attribute and share their ideas with the rest of the class. Suggestions will probably include legendary sports figures, exceptional cooks or eaters, artistic performers, or military figures. Focus on one or two characters and ask how a writer might develop a tall tale about the character: What would the greatest football player do to show his greatness? What would the best cook in the world do to show her skill? These questions will prompt students to invent the featured character and the context for their stories.

EPISODE 3.3.   Have students compose their tall tales in class while you offer your services as a consultant, providing individual feedback. As the stories develop, ask a few students to read their work aloud to the rest of the class. (Remember, tall tales come from an oral tradition.) You might also have students share their tales with one another in small groups.

Summing Up

Learning to write simple narratives introduces students to the basic elements: establishing setting and character, revealing characters' qualities through their actions, using vivid images, including dialogue, and conveying a theme. Now they are ready to study narratives written by more mature writers and write more complex narratives themselves.

Teaching Students to Write Narratives Collaboratively

Researchers Carl Bereiter and Marlene Scardamalia (1982) have demonstrated that what one does in conversation is not identical to what one does in writing. It is simplistic to suggest to students that writing is simply written speech. A *schema*, or generalized conception, for conversation is not reliable as the model for producing written text. Even though students' purposeful talk with one another is an important part of preparation for composition, the model of what one does in conversation is not the same as what one does in writing. Bereiter and Scardamalia noted that younger, inexperienced writers used a "what next" strategy when they worked independently: they wrote a little bit and then asked themselves, "What else can I say?" Without a conversational partner to prompt further production, these young writers quickly exhausted their efforts.

Mature writers employ a "means-end" strategy. They consider the goals they wish to accomplish and select what they judge the appropriate route to get there. They consider the many complicating factors that need to be addressed or the many needs of the audience that need to be satisfied. But here too it helps to have a partner or several partners who can ask key questions.

The lessons in this chapter help students develop means-end strategies by writing narratives collaboratively. Each of four examples connects with a specific work of literature, a particular genre, or a mode of literature (e.g., romance, comedy).

Begin by explaining that students will be writing a story together and noting a specific purpose—to learn about conventional narrative structures, to anticipate plot in their subsequent reading, to recognize a common pattern of narrative, or to develop procedures for producing a fairly complex narrative. While each group of students will focus on one episode, individual episodes will need to fit into the whole. To that end you'll need to prescribe the beginning and ending sentence for all the episodes. You might also note the implications of each episode and the need for resolutions.

Here is a step-by-step summary of the process:

1. Announce to the class that they will form teams to write a long story composed of several parts.

2. Set up small groups with the appropriate mix of males and females, extroverts and introverts, taskmasters and followers.

3. Explain that each group will receive a beginning and the ending sentence for one portion or phase of the story. Each sentence contains a detail of the story and the two sentences together suggest a narration that will connect the two details.

4. Assign a portion to each group.

5. Read aloud the beginning and ending sentence of each portion.

6. Answer questions about the process and the substance of the story portions.

7. Give each group a printed copy of the beginning and ending sentence of its assigned portion and set a time limit. (Formatting each handout with the beginning sentence at the top and the ending sentence at the bottom suggests they should write at least a page.)

8. Monitor the composing progress of each group, answering questions and offering encouragement.

9. When the parts are complete, have representatives from the groups read them aloud, in order.

10. Have the class discuss, and perhaps write about, how the story is similar to others they have read or have seen in films. Record their observations, introduce the term *romance of the hero*, and identify the pattern of this type of narrative.

The stories students produce will be relatively informal and unpredictable, and you should assess them accordingly: it would be inappropriate to set a narrow quality standard. A caution or two, however: students can get carried away with their own cleverness and invent irreconcilable events that undermine the efforts of the group. Nor should students merely imitate stories they see in popular television programs or resolve narrative problems *deus ex machina*. You keep students from falling into these traps by moving from group to group and checking their progress (step 8).

Stage 1. Writing a Hero Story Together

Students are likely to enjoy writing together with classmates, and they will practice a means-end strategy to produce their story. A further benefit is that they can compare their story with others that are similar. By the time students reach middle or high school, they have encountered several variations on the basic hero story. When students write their own hero story and compare it to others they have read, they can generalize about the pattern. In a sense, then, they define a mode of literature, the *romance of the hero*.

While writing the hero story, students solve narrative problems related to the genre's elements: the type of protagonist and his or her origins, the nature of the quest, the character of the villain or enemy, the pattern of the journey, the distinct challenges at each stage of the journey, and the ultimate struggle at the end. Afterward, they can speculate about why this narrative pattern persists. What makes it appealing to different cultures at vastly different times? How does the general pattern of the story function as a symbol, and as a symbol, what could it possibly represent?

`EPISODE 1.1:` **Introduce the narrative writing task.** Give students the set of sentences in Figure 2–1. Share the beginning and ending sentence for each part and ask students what the sentences suggest about the substance of the part. Here is a possible interchange about part 1:

Figure 2–1. "The Playground Bully": A Story in Six Parts

Part 1

Beginning sentence: When Shelley, Byron, and Keith parked their bikes and walked onto the playground, they came face to face with the bully who had been terrorizing students at John L. Lewis School since August.

Ending sentence: As the boy lifted himself from the ground, muddy saliva oozing from the corner of his mouth, Dillon jangled the loose change in his mud-caked fist.

Part 2

Beginning sentence: At lunch that day, Dillon leaned over their table and hissed, "I'll see you three after school."

Ending sentence: They pulled their bikes into Shelley's yard, panting softly and marveling about how they had outrun their menace.

Part 3

Beginning sentence: The next morning, the three friends stopped their bikes at the far end of the playground and puzzled how they would get to the bike rack and slip into school past Dillon, who stood with his arms crossed at the main entrance.

Ending sentence: They walked down the hall, safe for now, but they knew they could not get into school the same way every day.

Part 4

Beginning sentence: When Shelley emerged from her grandmother's basement apartment the next morning, she held in her hand a simple gift, a gift her grandmother claimed Shelley would value more every day.

Figure 2–1. "The Playground Bully": A Story in Six Parts (*continued*)

Ending sentence: They had escaped his grasp once again; this common object had liberated them from their tormentor.

Part 5

Beginning sentence: Two of Dillon's friends sat on the bike rack at Lewis School, apparently waiting for the three to arrive.
Ending sentence: Safely inside their classroom, they realized how lucky they were that help had arrived this time; but they knew that help would not always be there.

Part 6

Beginning sentence: As the three friends mounted their bikes and began to pedal away, Dillon and his two buddies stepped into their path.
Ending sentence: When it was all over, everyone appreciated that what Shelley, Byron, and Keith had done was difficult; life at John L. Lewis Elementary School would never be the same.

You: The first sentence says, "When Shelley, Byron, and Keith parked their bikes and walked onto the playground, they came face to face with the bully who had terrorized students at John L. Lewis School since August." The last sentence says, "As the boy lifted himself from the ground, muddy saliva oozing from the corner of his mouth, Dillon jangled the loose change in his mud-caked fist." What might have happened between the action suggested by the first sentence and the action suggested by the last sentence?

Tyler: I think that he pushed him down and he got all muddy.

Maggie: One of those guys—Shelley, Bryan, or Keith—got hit.

You: I wonder why the writer didn't use one of their names. It just says, "the boy." And who did the hitting?

Madison: It's that guy Dillon. I think what happened is that he took away the kid's lunch money.

You: How did that happen?

Maggie: I know, I know. He, Dillon, told this kid to give him his lunch money, but he didn't want to. So he made him give him the money.

You: What makes you think Dillon took the boy's money?

Maggie: He's jingling the money in his hand.

You: The boy, the victim, has muddy saliva coming from his mouth. How did mud get into his mouth?

Tyler: Dillon probably hit him when his hand was muddy. It says, "his mud-caked fist."

May: It says his *fist*, like he was fighting.

You: I see there are other hands up, but we have a lot of ideas, and we'll leave it up to the team to decide.

EPISODE 1.2: **Planning parts in groups.** Students, in small groups, begin to invent the story, evaluating the possibilities and trying out details. The following example, based on Part 6, is representative of the kind of *means-end* thinking they do to connect the beginning sentence logically to the ending sentence and honor the constraints represented by those sentences both for the individual part itself and the story as a whole.

Tyler: I'd like it to be a good situation if they go back to school, that they stood up to Dillon. If it's bad, they stood up to Dillon and they became the bullies themselves. They go down the path and one of them falls off his bike. . . .

Lauren: So, he falls off of his bike?

Tyler: They came to a stop real fast in front of the three boys.

Lauren: Do we know their names?

Tyler: I don't know. I picture them on the Prairie Path, and these guys jump out in front of them and they stand up to the bullies and then become bullies themselves.

Lauren: But how would everyone appreciate them? It says that everyone appreciated them.

Tyler: Yeah. We have to figure that out. Cam, what would you say for dialogue?

Cam: Like, "Oh, no, not these guys again."

Tyler: He could say, "We have some unfinished business." And he could remember about some bad thing that happened.

Lauren: Or he says something mean about someone.

Tyler: Cam, what could cause this big of a conversation?

Cam: They feel bad about being bullies, and they change.

Lauren: Would they say, "Get out of my way"?

Cam: Or a teacher could be coming down the path and helps them.

Tyler: Somehow they have to do something that's not violent but difficult to do.

Lauren: They could stand up to Dillon and say that they are tired of this and they are not going to put up with it any more. I like stories when the bully realizes that what he did was wrong.

Cam: That sounds like a good idea. He could be sorry and become friends with them.

Tyler: That way, the school will never be the same.

The narrative students produce will imitate to a certain extent the plot and theme in a hero story like *The Hobbit* or *The Wizard of Earthsea* or *The Odyssey*. Many students will find this an advantage when they read other hero narratives. The experience also helps them draw on their own knowledge and values when they encounter the themes and critical questions in a more mature narrative.

EPISODE 1.3: **Sharing the parts of the story.** Have a representative from each group read the group's part aloud, in order from 1 through 6. (Figure 2–2 is a story segment created by a student group.) Since the parts have been produced by groups working alone, they'll be a bit disjointed, which will both amuse the class and identify problems the writers need to correct as they revise and edit their efforts into one unified whole.

Figure 2–2. "Playground Bully"

Part 1

When Shelley, Byron, and Keith parked their bikes and walked onto the playground, they saw the bully who had been terrorizing the students at John L. Lewis School since August.

"What are we going to do now?" Shelley asked.

"Go get a cheeseburger from McDonald's?" Byron said.

"No, nugget. I mean about Dillon's bullying," Shelley responded.

"We can fight him ourselves," Keith suggested while pushing up his sleeves to show his muscles.

"Stop showing off," Shelley said. "I think we should just go talk to him."

"As much as both ideas sound good, I would rather not do either," Byron stated.

"Oh wa, wa. Grow up. It's the manly thing to do," Keith exclaimed.

"If you two would just stop and just look at what Dillon is doing," Shelley stated.

The three looked over at Dillon. "Give me your lunch money, twerp!" Dillon shouted. The boy looked at Dillon then looked down.

"I'd rather not," the boy muttered.

"Excuse me?" Dillon asked.

"I said no. Got a problem?" the boy asked confidently.

"As a matter of fact I do," Dillon shouted while cracking his knuckles. "I'll give you one more chance to give me that money or else!" Dillon exclaimed.

The boy looked into Dillon's firing eyes and finally stated sadly, "OK, I'll give you the money."

"Heh, heh, heh. That is the right choice, buddy," Dillon sassed.

Right as the boy was about to give Dillon the money, Shelley and Keith ran over shouting, "Whoa, stop right there."

"Yeah, stop right there," Byron added.

"A little late there, Byron," Shelley exclaimed.

"Anyways," Keith said, "don't give Dillon your money."

Figure 2–2. "Playground Bully" (*continued*)

"Excuse me. Don't listen to him," Dillon stated to the boy, pushing the three out of the way. The boy shivered with fear.

"Listen, Dillon, don't threaten him. At least take us," Shelley exclaimed.

"Well, I guess you look easier, especially meat loaf over there," Dillon stated.

"Hurtful," Byron uttered.

"Hey, don't call him meat loaf," Keith shouted.

"I can do whatever I want," Dillon added.

"You want to go?" Keith exclaimed while putting his fists up.

"Keith, stop," Shelley said.

"If you three would please leave, I have some finishing to do," Dillon stated. Dillon twisted the boy's arm around his back and took the boy's change. Dillon pushed the boy.

"Hey, we're going to tell a teacher!" Shelley exclaimed.

The three ran over to get a teacher. "This is the last and only time you're getting away," Dillon shouted to the three. He turned back to the boy, "What are you looking at, twerp?" Dillon exclaimed. And he pushed him into a big pile of mud.

As the boy lifted himself from the ground, muddy saliva oozing from the corner of his mouth, Dillon jangled the loose change in his mud-caked fist.

EPISODE 1.4. Have students join the episodes into a single story. As an alternative to a written story, you might help the students adapt the story into a script to act out and videotape.

Stage 2. Exploring Heroes and Fantasy

The collaborative hero story in Stage 1 is realistic fiction, but some hero tales take place in distant and exotic lands and include elements of magic and fantasy. This second example (see Figure 2–3) follows the same collaborative process as the first, but the entire first part of the story is provided; this collaborative writing experience prepares students for reading *Beowulf* or *The Once and Future King*.

Figure 2–3. "The Power and the Stone"

Phase 1

On a mild spring morning many years ago, a child was born in the town of Watermills, the capital of the tiny nation of Arboria. The parents, Carth and Rusa Heidro—two of the most respected citizens of Arboria—were delighted with their baby boy. They named him Yager and dreamed about the day when he would be a great man in Arboria. Their joy, however, did not last long.

Agorth, the King of Arboria, was a vain and superstitious man. Plans about how to retain his power occupied most of his thoughts. He worried little about attacks from other countries—Arboria was situated in a mountain range that historically had frustrated many foreign attacks—but he feared revolt from his own people, whom he kept on the verge of starvation in order to use what they produced to satisfy his own avarice.

Agorth often consulted Zethram, the court oracle, to receive comforting predictions about his continued reign over Arboria. During the year of Yager's birth, Zethram came to Agorth with a disturbing prediction. Appearing before the King, Zethram untied a cloth bag from his belt, removed a handful of small animal bones from the bag, and threw them on the floor at the feet of the King. Zethram stared coldly into Agorth's eyes and announced: "The meaning of the bones is clear. A child is born in this land who will end your reign over Arboria. A male child is born with a circle on his chest. He will grow in power until he brings down your rule."

The King was outraged. He threw down his goblet of wine and attacked the oracle. "Where is this child? Where?" he screamed, kicking and beating the oracle.

"The bones do not say, my lord!"

"He will have a circle on his chest? What does that mean? Where is such a child?"

"Perhaps, my lord, the child has a birthmark in the shape of a circle. Perhaps the parents have tattooed such a mark on the child, as some of the peasants do. Perhaps he wears a medallion in the shape of a circle. The bones do not say."

Figure 2–3. "The Power and the Stone" (*continued*)

King Agorth called for his ministers of defense and justice. He directed them to "search out a new born child in this land, a child with a circular mark or medallion on his chest. See that any such child is destroyed."

The ministers went forth to execute the king's bloody orders.

Phase 2

Beginning sentence: At dawn a contingent of heavily armed soldiers invaded the Heidro home to find the child whom their informers had identified.

Ending sentence: Instead the young soldier would take the child to his own parents, a poor peasant couple who lived on the banks of the Green River.

Phase 3

Beginning sentence: The child, whom the old peasant couple called Zed, had been with the couple for seventeen years, and in that time he thrived and became a masterful swineherd.

Ending sentence: Zed felt that he was too young and inadequate to accomplish this task, but the dark stranger recognized his hesitation and said, "Only you can act now, or Arboria will be awash with blood and tears."

Phase 4

Beginning sentence: This was the Skull Place that he had heard about many times during his childhood, but he must pass it if he were to continue his journey.

Ending sentence: As he continued some hundred yards along the mountain trail, Zed looked back at the fallen bodies and saw smoke rising from their hideous camp.

Phase 5

Beginning sentence: As often happens during the summer in the mountains, a raging storm swept over the passes, chasing Zed into the shelter of a deep cave.

(*continues*)

Figure 2–3. "The Power and the Stone" (*continued*)

Ending sentence: As Zed emerged from the tunnel, he examined the curious smooth round stone in his hand, wondering what secret magic it held.

Phase 6

Beginning sentence: Zed traveled for two more days before he reached his destination. He faced Agorth's towering black castle and wondered how he would enter without being captured.

Ending sentence: He then continued up the stone staircase toward the king's chamber and knew the power of the stone could not help him with what he had to do.

Phase 7

Beginning sentence: When Zed slowly opened the chamber door and viewed the powerful Agorth, he wished the dark stranger were now there to tell him what to do.

Ending sentence: The dark stranger appeared after the struggle had ended, noting the outcome and knowing that the kingdom would never be the same.

Stage 3. Writing a Comedy

Northrop Frye (1967) argues convincingly not only that comedies (especially the festive comedies of Shakespeare) have a common form but also that this form implies an argument: life triumphs over death, youth over old age, optimism over pessimism. In this lesson, a prelude to reading *As You Like It*, students respond to a set of prompts and write their own rough comedy. Their attempt gives them an insight into the writing of others, the work of Shakespeare in particular. The students define the characteristics of comedy as they discover them.

In the story, two young people are attracted to each other and vie to be together; an older and more narrow-minded person (a *senex*) tries to separate them; the problems of the young people become so thorny that they need to escape the community of older and more narrow-minded characters into a more pastoral setting or "green world"; matters become still more complicated as the young characters don disguises to protect themselves, resulting in cases of mistaken identity; the older characters follow the younger into the green world, bringing all parties together in a kind of Eden; problems work themselves out so that couples unite, differences are resolved, and all seem in harmony. Of course, the visitors cannot remain forever in the green world but must return to their proper society, where similar problems may recur.

The activity has two parts, so each group writes two portions of the story. They spend one class meeting writing the segments in Part 1 (see Figure 2–4), which lead the characters into the pastoral setting, and a second class meeting writing the segments that lead to the resolution of conflicts and the return to harmony (see Figure 2–5). A third class period may be needed to share all the segments.

Figure 2–4. "Escape to Greenfield Lake" (Part 1)

Segment 1

Beginning sentence: "Why can't I go to the spring dance?" Wally screamed at his Uncle Barry.

Ending sentence: Wally stormed out the front door, only to hear his uncle's thundering voice: "If you leave now, don't ever think about coming back!"

Segment 2

Beginning sentence: When Mr. Rodriguez arrived to pick up his daughter Carmelita from the dance, he saw her talking to two boys, one a new student at the school and the other a kid from the poorest area of town.

Ending sentence: After hearing what happened, Amelia assured her best friend, "Don't worry, Carmelita. No matter what your father says, we'll find a way for you to see Wally again."

Segment 3

Beginning sentence: The next morning Uncle Barry was the first one at the bank.

(continues)

Figure 2–4. "Escape to Greenfield Lake" (Part 1) (*continued*)

Ending sentence: Barry felt secure knowing that this deal would secure his future as an independent bachelor and take care of his insufferable nephew.

Segment 4

Beginning sentence: Wally looked at himself in the mirror and decided that this disguise could fool even Dennis.

Ending sentence: The sign said Greenfield Lake, but all Wally knew for sure was that this was where Dennis and he would stay until they could figure out their next move.

Segment 5

Beginning sentence: "How will we get there without anyone recognizing us?" Amelia asked.

Ending sentence: The girls walked out of the building, and Carmelita said, as if she knew it all along, "See, Amelia, dressed like this we could stay at the fishing resort for weeks."

Segment 6

Beginning sentence: It seemed that all the cabins were empty except for one, which had smoke rising from its chimney.

Ending sentence: When Wally and Dennis left the two young men, Wally couldn't help feeling they had met them before.

Or you might create and read the segments in Part 1 on one day, correct any inconsistencies, and then, on a second day, develop the segments for Part 2 in light of those changes. The students might note that the structure of the story has much in common with *Romeo and Juliet*, except for the happy ending. This realization could invite discussion about distinctions between comedy and tragedy and the implications for blending together elements of both into what might be seen as a "problem play."

Figure 2–5. "Escape to Greenfield Lake" (Part 2)

Segment 7

Beginning sentence: Sam Testaduro had been coming to Greenfield Lake for fifty years, but he had never before seen a sight like this—a woman apparently his own age, but so youthful, so innocent.

Ending sentence: Turning away from his advancing hand, Wally said, "It's quite late, Mr. Testaduro, and the fish won't wait for me in the morning."

Segment 8

Beginning sentence: Wally cautioned Dennis, "If you don't stop laughing, you're going to end up in the lake. You've got to help me."

Ending sentence: Wally felt a little more comfortable, knowing that he could rely on the young man to go along with the charade; but would Sam believe this strange-looking character could be the woman's lover and then leave him alone?

Segment 9

Beginning sentence: Uncle Barry drove his car slowly down the shaded lanes of the resort, looking for the cottage with the number 7 painted on a wooden partridge above the door.

Ending sentence: Uncle Barry pushed Sam away from the man with the moustache and said, "Sam Testaduro! What in the world are you doing?"

Segment 10

Beginning sentence: Sam was surprised to see Barry, the brother of his old partner on the police force.

Ending sentence: All this time Wally had been listening intently and now knew that the rumors about his father were untrue and that he still might be alive.

(continues)

Figure 2–5. "Escape to Greenfield Lake" (Part 2) (*continued*)

Segment 11

Beginning sentence: Feeling some glimmer of hope, Barry told Sam, "If you think you can trust your companions, there is a way we can help my brother and sister-in-law escape and make a new life."

Ending sentence: Barry turned to Sam and said, "Your girlfriend has a vicious right cross, but that guy with the moustache sure ran like a rabbit."

Segment 12

Beginning sentence: Mr. Rodriguez, whom everyone assumed to be dead, pulled in front of the lodge, along with three police cars.

Ending sentence: Carmelita hugged her father and said, "I'm glad we're staying for the Spring Blossom Dance, and you'll be my first partner—or maybe my second."

Stage 4. Writing a Collaborative Suspense Story

This activity is simpler than the previous two. It follows the same structure and process as the first activity. It can be used to introduce the much more involved suspense story described in the next chapter, which, although it involves a lot of student interaction, requires each student to produce a story independently. Writing this collaborative story first gives students the confidence that they can compose a story on their own.

Preview the collaborative writing task, read aloud the beginning and ending sentences for each portion of the story (see Figure 2–6), assign a portion to each group, and monitor the progress of all of the writers. The process begins with a great deal of guidance from you, continues with the collaborative efforts of small groups and the combined efforts of the class, and concludes with a more independent expression.

Figure 2–6. A Collaborative Suspense Story

Part 1

Beginning sentence: "Let's go in here," said Marcie, as she nudged open the door at the back of the school, hidden by a row of evergreens.

Ending sentence: As they slowly made their way down the dark hall, the four children realized that they were in a part of the school where they had never been before, and a part that they didn't know existed.

Part 2

Beginning sentence: Trying to sound calm, Pete said, "I don't think we should be in here, because we'll be in big trouble if someone finds us."

Ending sentence: Although Pete was still eager to get out of the school, he knew that they could not go back the way they came in, where they now could hear these strange sounds.

Part 3

Beginning sentence: "Quick, let's go down here," said Alison, pointing to a dark stairway that seemed to lead to a basement.

Ending sentence: Now that they looked around the room, Michael and the others froze in their footsteps, not believing what they saw.

Part 4

Beginning sentence: They felt a chill breeze sweep over them, causing the door to slam with a metallic bang, leaving the room in total darkness.

Ending sentence: "We are so lucky you had that with you, Pete," said Marcie, "or we would still be in that room."

Part 5

Beginning sentence: As they tip-toed up the stairs, each step seemed to echo, and they didn't know if they were hearing their own footfalls or the steps of someone else.

(continues)

> **Figure 2–6.** A Collaborative Suspense Story (*continued*)
>
> *Ending sentence*: Seeing a possible way out of the building now, they pledged that they would never tell anyone what they saw in the school.
>
> **Part 6**
>
> *Beginning sentence*: This one obstacle remained if they were to escape safely from the building, but how could they possibly do it?
>
> *Ending sentence*: Pointing back to the school, Marcie said, "Now that I know what is in there, I will never break into the school again."

The story in Figure 2–7 illustrates the type of work students typically produce.

> **Figure 2–7.** An Example of a Collaborative Suspense Story
>
> "Let's go in here," said Marcie, as she nudged open the door at the back of the school, hidden by a row of evergreens. "Look," she encouraged, "this is a secret way into the school."
>
> "No, we shouldn't go down there," said Alison. "We could get in trouble."
>
> "Yeah," said Pete.
>
> "You wimps," said Michael.
>
> "We're going in," said Marcie.
>
> Pete said, "Who are you calling a wimp?"
>
> Challenged in this way, Michael and Pete followed Marcie into the school. Alison sighed and went inside the building after them.
>
> After they got in, the door slammed shut behind them. It was pitch dark. They felt their way down the

Figure 2–7. An Example of a Collaborative Suspense Story (*continued*)

wall. They felt what seemed like lichens and mosses. They knew nobody had been down there for a long time. Pete suddenly tripped. He rubbed his knee and groaned from pain. Pete felt around the floor to find what had tripped him. He discovered that he had tripped on a flashlight. Alison heard a metal clink. "W-what's that?" stammered Alison.

"I found it when I tripped," said Pete.

Marcie felt around. "Hey, I think I found a switch." Marcie pulled the switch, hoping she was turning on a light. Instead, a trap door opened under them. They all screamed in terror as they slid down a ramp, landing with a splash in a shallow pool of filthy water.

"What h-happened?" said Michael in terror and disgust. The four friends stood and shook the fetid water off their arms and hands, as best they could.

They saw a dry hallway and limped forward. The hall was dimly lit. When they looked into an adjoining room, they saw desks, tables, and what appeared to be a pile of math books. "Hey," said Marcie in a frightened tone, "I saw something move in that pile."

"Let's keep moving," said Michael.

As they slowly made their way down the dark hall, the four children realized that they were in a part of the school where they had never been before, and a part that they didn't know existed.

Trying to sound calm, Pete said, "I don't think we should be in here, because we'll be in big trouble if someone finds us."

"No. I'm curious," said Michael.

They all froze when they heard creaking footsteps. Then they started walking toward the sound and heard a big scream echoing from a distant part of the school.

(*continues*)

Figure 2–7. An Example of a Collaborative Suspense Story (*continued*)

They walked toward the sound and found a decomposing human body. They grabbed each other, unable to move. But Marcie gathered her courage and stepped forward. "We have to find out who it is," she said. Marcie crept forward, looking for signs that might help her to recognize the victim. "I think I know that tie," she said, "and his suit looks familiar."

Moving closer, Marcie noticed a name badge pinned to the man's suit. She bent down to read it and knew in an instant that the dead body was that of their old principal Mr. Huffenclocher. "It's Mr. Huffenclocher!" she cried. "What could have happened to him? We've got to get out of here!"

They all turned and ran away, screaming in terror, but when they lurched down the dark hall, they suddenly hit a door and fell to the ground. Pete reached up and opened the door just as they heard another blood-curdling scream.

Although Pete was still eager to get out of the school, he knew that they could not go back the way they came in, where they now could hear these strange sounds.

"Quick, let's go down here," said Alison, pointing to a dark stairway that seemed to lead to a basement.

Slowly and silently they all went down the stairs. When they got to the bottom, they were amazed. The basement was filled with Halloween decorations, including a collection of huge jack-o'-lanterns. As they started to examine the decorations, Pete yelled, "Help!" Through the dim light they saw Pete being dragged out of the room by a jack-o'-lantern that had grown legs, arms, and fangs. "Pete!" they yelled. But Pete was gone.

Marcie, Michael, and Alison started after Pete, but a glowing skeleton jumped in front of them. He extended his long arm and hand to grab Marcie and pull her toward him. They watched helplessly as the skeleton

Figure 2–7. An Example of a Collaborative Suspense Story (*continued*)

pulled her into the same room into which Pete had disappeared. Michael and Alison followed into the room. They thought it was a storage closet, but then the lights went on.

Now that they looked around the room, Michael and Alison froze in their footsteps, not believing what they saw.

They felt a chill breeze sweep over them, causing the door to slam with a metallic bang, leaving the room in total darkness.

They had an uneasy feeling in their stomachs. "What happened?" asked Alison. "Shhh! We don't want anybody to hear us," said Marcie. "Hang on. I think I still have the flashlight in my pocket," said Pete.

Alison and Michael were shocked and relieved that Pete and Marcie were still with them. "Okay, let's have a look around," said Michael.

"Let's split up," said Marcie.

"Hey, look what I found," said Michael, pointing to a key on a hook. In the dust on the floor below the key, someone had written, "This key can only work once in any lock; then it will disappear. Be careful!"

"Okay, thanks," said Alison.

"Let's pick it up and try it," said Michael. He slowly slipped it into the door at the end of the room and said, "Yes, it fits. Let's get out of here!" They all went through the doorway and headed down a new hallway, where they could see a stairway at the end.

"We are so lucky you had that flashlight with you, Pete," said Marcia, "or we would still be in that room."

As they tip-toed up the stairs, each step seemed to echo, and they didn't know if they were hearing their own footfalls or the steps of someone else.

(continues)

Figure 2–7. An Example of a Collaborative Suspense Story (*continued*)

"Uh-oh, we've messed up now," said Pete. As they quickly moved forward, all of a sudden Marcie screamed because something grabbed her. Then everyone started laughing. Michael had tricked her by grabbing her arm.

"You scared me!" said Marcie.

"Okay, everyone, no fooling around," insisted Alison. So as they walked through the hall they heard the creaking wood floor from behind. They froze in place and slowly turned around and saw some glowing object. It appeared to be the ghost of Mr. Zeithaule, the crazy old science teacher. There was a legend that he had turned himself into a mouse and got caught by a mouse trap. He died saying, "I am going to get revenge on all the people who mocked me."

Alison screamed, as she felt something grab her leg. "Hey, no fooling around," she said. But it was no joke! Something actually got her. "Guys, help me! Something gooey is pulling me away!"

Quickly they grabbed Alison and pulled her as hard as they could until Alison got loose. Once they got Alison, they ran as fast as they could down the hall toward the dim light, but they continued to hear a hideous laugh behind them.

Seeing a possible way out of the building now, they pledged that they would never tell anyone what they saw in the school.

This one obstacle remained if they were to escape safely from the building, but how could they possibly do it?

The noises started to get louder. "Did you hear that?" asked Pete.

"Hear what?" said Alison.

"Those noises!" said Pete.

Figure 2–7. An Example of a Collaborative Suspense Story (*continued*)

"I'm scared!" said Michael. They continued walking forward. Then they saw an old man. "Hey, kids," he said, "I can show you the way out."

Encouraged, the four friends moved toward the old man. As they got closer, he seemed to fade more and more. "How did you know we were trying to get out?" asked the kids all together. But he faded entirely before they could reach him. But they could see an open window ahead.

They all squeezed through the window and made a short jump to the ground. They were so glad to be outside again, where they could breathe the fresh air, far from the horrors they had just seen.

Pointing back to the school, Marcie said, "Now that I know what is in there, I will never break into the school again."

3

Teaching Students to Write a Suspense Story

This chapter presents a series of lessons preparing students to write a suspense story. The lessons are geared to younger writers but, with simple adjustments, can be used with older students as well.

Task Analysis

Your explicit goal: *students will produce suspense stories that use descriptive details and logical development to create the appropriate mood and elicit an empathic response from the reader.* Your students are likely familiar with suspense stories as a kind of narrative and have probably thought up subjects and situations for their own stories in the past. You will use the following materials to help them tap into this prior knowledge:

- A set of stories that will help the students to define the genre.

- A photo of a deserted alley (Figure 3–1), preferably on a transparency or video monitor.

- Sound recordings of cars coming and going on wet pavement, footsteps advancing and retreating, and metallic rattling produced by a dumpster lid opening and closing. (These sounds are available on standard sound effects recordings, many of which are available for free online, or can easily be captured with a handheld audio recorder.)

- A means of playing these recordings.

Figure 3–1. A Deserted Alley

Stage 1. Generating Criteria for Assessing Suspense Stories

EPISODE 1.1.   Tell your students they will read and discuss a number of stories in class and then, over a series of days, write a story of their own that has many of the same features. Volunteers will read their completed stories to the class, and copies of all their stories will remain in the classroom or in the school library or on the class website for future students to enjoy.

Read the stories in Figures 3–2, 3–3, and 3–4 aloud. Have students, in groups of three or four, (1) list the features that the three stories have in common and (2) rank the stories from best to worst.

Figure 3–2. Story 1

My aunt came to visit us and stay at our house for the weekend. When my aunt came into the house, she left her heavy suitcase at the top of the landing that leads to the basement. Later that night, when my mom and my aunt were drinking tea and talking at the kitchen table, they thought they heard someone pounding on our back door. My mom and aunt freaked out, because no one usually knocks on the back door.

They were afraid to open the back door, so they got a flashlight and shined it out of the window and into the backyard. Finally, my mom got our little dog (9 pounds) and set the phone to speed dial 911. My mom went out the front door and searched around the house to see if she could find who was pounding on the door. She couldn't see anyone.

When Mom came in again, my aunt asked where her suitcase was. We saw that it was at the bottom of the stairs to the basement. It fell down the stairs and must have made a pounding noise that made us think that someone was banging on the back door.

Figure 3–3. Story 2

We heard the sound of "crunch, crunch, crunch" coming from behind us in the dark woods that surrounded our campsite. Suddenly my heart pounded in my chest like a hammer banging against a wall. "What's that?" I asked my dad and my friend Chris.

Chris said nothing, but my dad tried to be calm: "It was probably a dead tree limb that fell in the woods, or it may be some little animal like a squirrel."

I stood up and looked around. "No, Dad. It sounded like something a lot heavier than a squirrel. What do you

Figure 3–3. Story 2 (*continued*)

think it could be?" I tried to look into the dark woods, but the light from our campfire couldn't penetrate the dark around the trees. I stood in a small circle of light, with the darkness surrounding us.

"If it will make you feel better," my dad said, "I'll take a look."

He got up from his seat on a log near the fire and grabbed a flashlight. The thought of my dad going into the woods alone and leaving Chris and me behind paralyzed me. "Wait, Dad. Let's listen to hear it again."

By now, Chris was standing, too. The three of us stood close by the fire, casting long narrow shadows that reached into the darkness of the woods. The fire hissed and popped, and the breeze moved smoke from the fire to wrap around us. Breezes stirred dead leaves that seemed to chase after each other and dance in circles. As we tried to be as still as possible, my heart raced and rushed blood to my ears, making a muffled booming noise. I heard something else, which could have been Chris whimpering.

"This is silly," said Dad. "I'm going to see if there is anything there."

Once my dad has made up his mind, there is no stopping him. He moved quickly into the woods, with the hazy beam of light from his flashlight leading the way.

Chris finally spoke. "Maybe we should wait in the truck," he said.

I agreed, but I didn't want to seem too panicked. "Let's just wait here by the fire," I said.

We stood there for a long time, and the fire was beginning to die down. I put a couple of small logs on the fire, to keep up the light and to give me something to do. My dad was gone for a long time. Then I heard the "crunch, crunch, crunch" again. "Chris, did you hear that?" I asked.

(continues)

Figure 3–3. Story 2 (*continued*)

"I hear something walking toward us," said Chris. You could see him tense up, like a hedgehog rolling itself into a ball. I think that if we were a little bit younger, he would have grabbed my arm for support.

"Is that you, Dad?" I called out. No answer. "Dad, we're over here," I shouted.

"Yeah, we're over here," Chris yelled. No answer.

We looked into the woods all around us. It was like trying to read something at the bottom of a cup of coffee. In the distance we saw a dim light dancing around. "Look. What's that?" I asked Chris.

"I don't know, but I wish your dad was back."

I went to the truck and got another flashlight from the glove compartment. I started to flash it in the direction of the other light, moving the light back and forth. The light in the woods also moved back and forth as if to imitate my movement. As I watched, the light in the woods seemed to get closer and closer. I wanted that light to be my dad returning to the campsite, but I wasn't sure. I grabbed Chris by the shoulder and we moved to the far side of the campsite and waited.

We watched the light move closer and closer, until Dad finally came out of the woods and into the glow of the campfire. "Thank goodness you flashed that flashlight into the woods. I lost my way back to the campsite and I thought I'd have to make a bed on the leaves in the woods. You helped me find my way back. But I couldn't find anything out there, so let's put out the fire and go to bed."

We were so happy to see my dad return and so relieved that we were glad to crawl into our sleeping bags. With the campfire out, there was no more hiss and pop, and the breeze died down. Dad and Chris quickly went to sleep in the tent. I was just about to fall asleep myself, when I heard, "crunch, crunch, crunch."

Figure 3–4. Story 3

There was an old woman who lived in my neighbor-hood. My friends and I didn't know her name. She looked really old. She wore ragged old clothes. No matter what the weather, her outdoor clothes always included a scarf and a heavy cloth overcoat with a wide and ragged collar. The rumor in the neighborhood was that she was a witch.

She lived in a wooden frame house, one-story with an attic. All the windows were covered, with news-papers or curtains or even boards. It would be impos-sible to look in, even if one had the courage to do it. The house hadn't been painted in years, and it looked gray and brown and weather-beaten, almost like the old woman herself. Everyone knew that the house was filled with hundreds of stray dogs and cats. No one saw the woman walk a dog or sit on her porch with a cat in her lap, but you could see her buying a lot of pet food at the supermarket. And even outside the house it smelled like animal waste.

One afternoon, as I passed her house with a couple of my friends, my buddy Dennis said, "Watch this." He then walked up the three steps to the old woman's wooden porch and jumped up and down. The banging on the wooden porch set off an uproar of dog howls, cat screams, scrambling paws, overturned furniture, and scraping claws. There was no way to tell the number of animals inside the house, but it sounded as if there were hundreds. The house fairly rocked with the barks and cries. It was like having a live, wild door bell.

We moved a few yards away from the house and waited for the noise to stop. Dennis then went back to the porch and pounded on it again. There was another uproar. The windows rattled, and the door shook un-der the weight of dozens of dogs hurtling themselves against it.

(continues)

Figure 3–4. Story 3 *(continued)*

Soon the noise stopped again; then Dennis approached me and said, "Why don't you try it?" I wasn't sure. The first time might have caught the old woman by surprise. The second time might also have caught her by surprise, with the woman thinking, "No one would pull the same prank twice." At the third attempt she might be waiting, maybe preparing to unleash several attack dogs.

I slowly began walking up the creaking wooden stairs. As I reached the second step, Dennis half-whispered, "I'll watch the windows and the back." I hadn't thought about needing a lookout. As I crouched to begin my jump, Dennis yelled, "She's coming out the back! She's got two dogs!"

I leaped over the rail of the porch and began running in the direction where Dennis had already fled. I knew that if the old lady were leading dogs on a leash, they would never come close to catching us. But I worried about her unleashing the dogs, and I believed that I heard the panting of dogs and the scraping of claws on the concrete walk behind me. I ran all the way home and into my yard. I closed the fence gate behind me and gasped for breath. But I didn't see or hear any dogs.

Two days later, I was at the grocery store with my mom. While my mom was at the deli counter, the old woman came up to me as I leaned against the shopping cart and whispered, "I'll get you next time."

EPISODE 1.2. Have representatives from each group share the group's list of common features and story rankings. In a whole-class discussion, come up with a list of the basic features of a suspense story, as well as features that distinguish a good story from a weak one. (You might ask, What do the stories have in common? How did you make your decisions about what makes a good story?) Rephrase student suggestions and filter their contributions as necessary. For example, if a student says that all three stories involve animals, you might ask, "Is that *coincidental* or *essential* to all of the stories? Do all stories of this kind have to have animals in them?" Your list of the essential elements in a suspense story will probably include:

There is something weird or unknown.

Something or someone poses a threat to the main character.

The main character feels frightened or threatened.

The reader worries that something bad might happen to the main character.

There is enough descriptive detail for the reader to imagine the characters, setting, and action.

The events of the story occur in a logical order.

Dialogue is often included. (You may have to add this item yourself, define it, and talk about how it adds immediacy.)

Tell students they are going to write a similar type of story and that it must include all these elements. (In other words, the elements are the criteria you will use to grade the stories.) Add these two constraints to the assignment:

1. The story must be realistic enough to give the reader the feeling that the events could happen to anyone. Avoid wild exaggerations, supernatural interventions, and outrageous parodies.

2. Downplay violence. The suspense should derive from the sense of dread or foreboding, not from machine guns, bombs, or knives.

Stage 2. Prewriting

EPISODE 2.1. Darken the classroom and project Figure 3–1. Ask students to suggest all the words they can think of that might appear in a story set in this alley. Encourage them to include action words.

After a couple of minutes, call on volunteers to share their words. Here's a sample:

Word List

drip	alarm
footsteps	bouncing
creaky	door closing
clump	creaking
splash	echoes
puddle	horrible
alley cat	pop out
screech	rattle
racing cars	flies
v-roooom	buzzing
slamming doors	skunk
scream	rotten eggs
high pitched	body
siren	damp
mist	fog

Creating this list gets students thinking about the substance of a suspense story, helps them come up with a plot, and provides a convenient word bank from which to draw when writing descriptions.

EPISODE 2.2.   Ask each student to imagine that he or she (or an invented character) is alone and crouched between two of the dumpsters. Play a recording of street noises: cars coming and going, a dog pattering by, footsteps on wet pavement growing louder and more distinct as they approach. Have students jot down ideas about other sounds they might hear in the alley, the smells around them, and the emotions they would experience.

EPISODE 2.3. Prompt students to write a description of the setting: Help your reader see, hear, smell, and feel whatever the character would be feeling in the situation. In your description, bring the setting to life. Rely on vivid verbs and striking comparisons. Keep in mind some of the words and phrases in our word bank.

Give students about fifteen minutes to write their descriptions, then ask volunteers to share. Point out effective verb choices and comparisons, and encourage everyone to pay special attention to the verbs and comparisons they use.

EPISODE 2.4. Have students, in groups of three, discuss possible scenarios beginning with a stranger approaching someone—for example, a dreaded enemy seeking revenge, a law enforcement officer searching for an escapee, or a mobster coming to bump off a rival. Students, while stating possibilities, agreeing or disagreeing, suggesting variations, adding details, or questioning whether a situation is feasible, begin to generate and refine the story.

Stage 3. Drafting the Narratives

EPISODE 3.1. Call students' attention to the first paragraph in each of the three example stories. One story begins with a sound and an action, one describes the setting, and one describes a character. Ask which opening appeals to them most as readers. Remind them they have many options for how to begin their story.

EPISODE 3.2. Model how a writer uses and punctuates dialogue. Show students how to convert indirect quotations to direct quotations, where to place end punctuation in relation to quotation marks, and how to begin a new paragraph to indicate a shift in speaker.

EPISODE 3.3. Have each student begin drafting a story, paying special attention to details that will bring the situation and setting to life. (They can continue to work on the story at home.)

Stage 4. **Editing**

EPISODE 4.1. Model reworking a draft. Project a transparency of a former student's draft essay (name removed). Check that it has all the features essential to a suspense story. Strengthen the verbs, insert some comparisons, edit the dialogue.

EPISODE 4.2. Have students exchange drafts with a partner and recommend editorial changes and revisions based on what they need to know as readers. Have them follow this procedure:

1. The writer slowly reads the story aloud to his/her partner.

2. Each partner tells the other, "The thing I liked most about your story was. . . ."

3. Each partner points out any missing essential elements.

4. Each student then reads his/her partner's story silently and (with the writer's permission) corrects errors in spelling, punctuation, and indentation.

EPISODES 4.3 AND/OR 4.4. Have students revise one or two more drafts, each time with different partners.

Stage 5. **Publishing the Narratives**

Ask a few volunteers to read their story aloud to the class (or to let you read it for them). Then gather a copy of every student's story into a class book. You could also have teams of students dramatize their stories or perform them as reader's theater pieces. Figures 3–5 and 3–6 are examples of typical stories written by fifth graders.

Stage 6. **Encouraging Student Reflection**

After a few days, tell students how impressed you were by their work and ask them to write a brief letter to you explaining what helped

Figure 3–5. "Lost Dog," by Sarah Knighton

I was rushing to get ready! It was cold out and my mom told me I had to wear layers of clothes. I hate wearing layers of clothes but I had to obey my mom, unfortunately! It looked like it was about to rain. Every Halloween I had to go trick-or-treating with my mom, but at least this year I got to go with my friends, too. I go to my grandma's almost every Halloween before I go trick-or-treating. It stinks because my grandma lives all the way in Chicago. I told my mom that I was ready and we started on our way to Chicago. I was looking out the window when I noticed it was getting really dark out and it started to rain. My grandma lives in an apartment by an alley. We finally got there and I ran into the apartment because I didn't want to get my costume wet. My mom had parked the car and came inside by me. Then I rang the doorbell. I saw the light turn on and I could hear my grandma's footsteps.

My grandma said, "Who is it?"

I said, "Grandma, it's me."

She opened the door and said, "Oh, it's my little clown!" I smiled. She said that because I was a clown for Halloween. We got inside and sat down in the living room. My stomach was making a funny noise. I asked my grandma if I could have something to eat. She nodded her head and continued to talk to my mom. So I went to the kitchen and grabbed the last packet of fruit snacks. I went over to throw out the box when I noticed that the garbage can was full. I told my grandma and she asked me if I could take the garbage out. I hesitated and said, "Well, okay."

I didn't want to go because the dumpster was in the alley and it was dark out. I walked outside, I was nervous and I was getting the goose bumps. I got into the alley and felt a rain drop dripping down my forehead. My

(continues)

Figure 3–5. "Lost Dog," by Sarah Knighton (*continued*)

knees were shaking. I threw out the bag. I heard something and looked over my left shoulder, I saw a dog. The
dog was dripping wet and smelled very bad. She was
very small and was limping so I think her leg was broken.
I think she was afraid of me because she was slowly back-
ing away. I heard footsteps coming toward me. I quickly
grabbed the dog and hid in between the two dumpsters.

I heard a voice. "Roxie!" the voice called.

"Yikes!" I whispered.

I could hear the footsteps slowly going away. I peeked
out into the alley. I couldn't see anyone. I slowly walked
to the apartment door. I walked inside thinking of what
to say to my mom. I looked down at the dog, and she
was shivering.

I shouted to my mom from the kitchen, "Mom, can I
see you in the kitchen?"

She said, "I will be there in a minute."

My heart was beating so fast, I felt like it was going
to jump out of my body. My mom finally came in and I
quickly said something before she could yell at me.

I said, "You see, Mom, I was taking out the garbage
and I saw this dog. It looked like it was hurt so I picked it
up. Please, oh, please, can I keep it!"

My mom looked puzzled. Then she said, "Did you
hear anything or see anything in the alley?"

I didn't want to tell my mom. I knew I had to, though.

Slowly I said, "Well, I did hear footsteps and someone
call the name Roxie." I looked down, thinking that I was
holding Roxie. There was a long silence; then my mom
said, "Why don't we go back to the alley and see if the
person is still there." I agreed.

We walked down to the alley together. I got the goose
bumps again.

My mom said, "Well, I guess we have to keep her." I
smiled. I looked down at Roxie but she wasn't there.

Figure 3–6. "Never Coming Back," by Perri Brinkmeier

Amy and Peter were walking back from the local coffee shop at 9:00 at night. It was cold, rainy, and mysterious. They were planning on taking the long way home just when Amy said, "Let's take the short cut through the alley."

"That creepy thing?" Peter asked. "Are you sure it won't be long?"

"It won't be more than two minutes," Amy explained.

"Are you sure?" Peter asked nervously.

"You're just a chicken!" Amy taunted.

"I am not!" Peter shouted and went unhappily along with Amy.

Peter took his first steps into the alley. The wind started to howl and Peter stuttered, "I'm going back!"

Amy stopped him. "Oh, come on. You'll be fine."

They were in the middle of the alley when they heard glass breaking. They looked up and in one of the windows of the apartment building they saw a man in black clothes and a black mask holding a bag.

"Aaaaahhhhhhhhhhhh," they screamed. The man in black heard them and ran down the back stairs chasing them. He dropped the black bag, but didn't notice it. Amy and Peter kept running until they went around the corner and found a place to hide. The man ran past them and Peter whispered intensely, *"I'm going home!"*

"Why? Isn't this fun? We can look at what he hid in the bag!" Amy questioned.

"No, you were wrong once and you're going to be wrong again!" Peter whispered angrily.

"Fine. I'll stay here alone! You go home!"

"I will," Peter said and started running home. Amy walked back to get the bag, but the man was coming back!

(continues)

Figure 3–6. "Never Coming Back," by Perri Brinkmeier (*continued*)

"What will I do?" Amy said to herself. She hid between two dumpsters and watched what the mystery man did.

"Where's the bag?" the guy whispered to himself. Amy heard a voice, but the man's lips weren't moving. There must be another man. Amy thought she heard his name was Rob.

Rob whispered, "Who's the jewelry from?"

"Mrs. Gory," said the other man in his dark voice. "She's like 85 years old and she lives by herself. Let's go back to Mrs. Gory's house tomorrow night."

They finally left. Amy thought they never would. It really stinks between those dumpsters.

Later that night Amy called Mrs. Gory to warn her about the two men who were going to come the next night. Amy asked Mrs. Gory if she would like her to be there.

Mrs. Gory called the police station. "I want to report a robbery. My jewels were stolen last night. And they are coming back tonight to steal more!"

The police were interested. "We will *definitely* be there! Wait for us."

Mrs. Gory was writing all this down so she could remember.

That night, Amy and Mrs. Gory were waiting for the police to come. Minutes passed, hours passed, and they were still waiting. Mrs. Gory went up to the door and listened. She heard voices and recognized them from the police department, so she opened the door to let them in.

But instead of the police, Mrs. Gory and Amy saw two men wearing black. And that was the end of Mrs. Gory and Amy.

them write such good stories. By thinking about their process like this, students realize they can rely on these same techniques to produce other narratives. Below are three examples of student responses:

> I relished the sounds that you had on the tape and the sounds you helped us come up with. But most of all, I enjoyed making the story. As you know, it is always hard to get started. But once you've started, you get the idea and you can keep going. . . . One thing that I didn't think was necessary was the picture of the alley. It was helpful a little bit. Although, I bet we still could have imagined it.
>
> —*Kerri*

> I liked when you played the sound! That really gave me my idea of a man walking through an alley taking very slow steps. The picture gave me an idea of what the setting of my story would be like! Those three stories you read us helped a lot! Now I know that a scary story is not about violence but is about getting the reader's heart pounding.
>
> —*Maggie*

> The three stories helped me know what the story should be like. Sharing our ideas in a small group was fun. It helped me develop a base idea for the story.
>
> —*Eric*

Summing Up

These lessons begin with a task analysis. Who are your learners and what do they already know about content and procedures that will help them do what you are asking them to do? What makes a narrative? Elements include having a story to tell; drawing on personal experiences to develop the story; recognizing the specific form, conventions, and quality standard for the specific genre; and generating detailed descriptions and narration. How should you structure the lessons? You'll want to prompt interest; help students generate ideas; show them how to plan and draft their story; help them review, assess, and refine their efforts; and provide a way they can share their story with their peers.

One lesson template does not fit every situation. You'll need to react and adjust along the way. Instructional design is organic; you need to follow new paths and pacing as the lessons progress, adjust to the specific circumstances. Share and plan with colleagues, who can ask questions and offer suggestions and variations. Observe one another teach. A collegial approach benefits everyone on the team.

Using Visual Images to Generate Stories

Teachers have long known that using visual images as prompts is a great way to get students to write description and narration. If a picture is worth a thousand words, then it should inspire students to put those thousand words down on paper. But you can't simply display a picture and tell students to write a story about it. Some pictures are better than others in evoking a story, and telling a story involves more than recounting a series of events. Stories create settings and characters in a way that lets the reader imagine a time and place and the people who populate that place. Characters come alive in part because of what a narrator says about them but also because of what they do and say. The action of a story conveys a vision of the world, perhaps moving from complication to complication and on to a happy resolution, or moving through a series of fortunate occurrences before declining suddenly into catastrophe. Descriptive words, the pattern of events, the language and actions of the characters, and the resolution all conspire to convey a mood, create an effect, or deliver a message.

The first two lessons that follow use celebrated American paintings (not reproduced here) and related prompts to encourage students to generate the conventional features of stories and plan logical relationships among incidents and events. (Illustrated books, including books produced primarily for children, are another source of powerful images; the works of Chris Van Allsburg, Jerry Pinkney, or Leo and Diane Dillon are excellent examples.) The third lesson uses photographs, which *are* reproduced; you can of course use others. More important than the specific images is the structure of the activities, which helps students formulate descriptive details that make characters, setting, and actions come alive.

While your first step may be selecting a picture or pictures to prompt storytelling, you then need to structure ways to encourage students to include the features readers find appealing about stories.

Stage 1. Creating Narratives Based on the Work of American Realist Painters

American Realist paintings typically evoke narration. The detailed, vivid images in the paintings of Bellows, Whistler, Sloan, and Eakins, for example, suggest a story to the viewer. These images can prompt students to narrate an incident; they can also challenge them to link one image to another, uniting a series of incidents into one longer, coherent story.

However, students must learn to see the frame of the picture as a window into another world: they shouldn't refer to the painting directly or refer to themselves as viewing the painting. For example, rather than, "In this painting I see two guys in a row boat on a river," one might say, "The scull cut a white crease through the murky waters of the Charles River, its crewmen straining against the wind and current." Students will need you to model what you expect and will benefit from talking with their classmates about what they see and imagine going on in the image.

This activity lends itself to collaboration. You can divide the class into teams, have each team create a narration suggested by one image, then ask all the teams to link their specific incidents into a unified whole. Or have each team create narratives for all the images and then connect them into a coherent story.

It's great if you can display fairly large reproductions of the paintings in the classroom, but you can also find the images online and project enlarged versions everyone can see or have students call up the images on individual computers.

The series of questions that accompany each image prompt students to describe the scene and/or characters and imagine related events and actions; if you are linking a series of images, the prompts encourage a coherent story. The episodes below provide a framework, but you will need to orchestrate procedures for generating ideas, planning, drafting, sharing, and refining.

Have students follow this process:

1. *Speculation*: A first step is for each writer to speculate on his or her own about the answers to the prompts in order to have something to contribute to the subsequent group work.

2. *Interaction*: Interaction among the writers encourages the structure of the narrative. Each team, working together, tries out possibilities for each image and for the combination of images. Each team member records these ideas to use as a guide when writing her or his draft.

3. *Draft*: Each student drafts a narrative that has these components:

    a. enough description to allow the reader to imagine the settings, characters, and events

    b. a series of connected events leading to a climax or resolution of a conflict

    c. dialogue capturing conversations among the characters in the story

    d. a theme, message, or prevailing feeling or effect conveyed through a logical sequence of events or pattern of actions and/or images

4. *Revising and editing*: Each writer meets with a reader (you or a classmate). Together they reflect on the quality of the narrative, keeping the basic components in mind and discussing possibilities for revising the story for clarity, coherence, and consistency.

5. *Publishing*: Each writer produces a finished product.

EPISODE 1.1. *The Cliff Dwellers*, by George Bellows, is part of the collection at the Los Angeles County Museum of Art (LACMA) and can be viewed online at http://collectionsonline.lacma.org/mweb cgi/mweb.exe?request=record;id=12254;type=10. Give students the following prompts:

1. Focus on one action in this scene. Begin the story by reporting the action. This might be dialogue that you overhear, an action that you can see, or behavior you can imagine happening at this time but that is out of view at the moment.

2. Describe the *whole scene* for your reader. What do you hear, smell, see, and feel?

3. The main character of your story is somewhere in this scene. Who is the character? Describe the character in detail. What is the character's vantage point? What is the character doing?

4. The central character will experience some *conflict*. Suggest some idea of the conflict. Keep in mind the subsequent images.

EPISODE 1.2. *White Girl*, by James McNeill Whistler (image is available on the Paris Web Museum at www.ibiblio.org/wm/paint/auth /whistler/i/white-girl.jpg). Give students the following prompts:

1. Who is this character? Describe her completely: her appearance, her personality, her voice, her smell. What does her dress and manner reveal about her?

2. Describe the setting. If you could look around the room she's in, what else would you see? What does the setting reveal about the character's life?

3. What connection does this character have to the previous scene? What are her plans, dreams, and feelings? If you could enter her mind, what thoughts would she reveal in an *interior monologue*?

4. Focus your description of place on some object as a *symbolic representation* of the character or her condition.

5. What part does this character play in the central conflict of the narrative?

EPISODE 1.3. *McSorley's Bar*, by John Sloan (image is available at http://commons.wikimedia.org/wiki/File:McSorley's_Bar_1912_ John_Sloan.jpg). Give students the following prompts:

1. Describe the scene: What do you smell? What background sounds do you hear? What can you see? Compare the scene (its looks, sound, and/or smell) to something else that captures its essence.

2. Who are the characters? Focus on two characters in particular. Think about their connection to previous and to subsequent scenes. The characters are obviously engaged in conversation. What are they talking about? Represent their conversation in dialogue.

3. Do other characters enter and leave the scene? If so, describe their physical appearance and their behavior.

4. How does the conversation end? How do details in the conversation complicate the central conflict of the story?

EPISODE 1.4. *The Biglen Brothers Racing*, by Thomas Eakins, is part of the collection of the National Gallery of Art and can be viewed at www.nga.gov/collection/gallery/gg68/gg68-42848-exhibit.html. Give students the following prompts:

1. Describe the setting. Given the setting, what do you smell and hear? What *new* comparisons can you make to help a reader sense the sounds and smells?

2. Who are the characters? Describe them. How are they related to each other?

3. Describe the action of the scene. The picture captures a moment. What has been happening? What will continue

to happen? Why are the characters doing what they
are doing?

4. How are the characters and their actions connected to
    previous and subsequent scenes?

5. How does this individual scene fit into the plot as a whole?

EPISODE 1.5. *Stag at Sharkey's*, by George Bellows, is part of the collection at the Cleveland Museum of Art, available for viewing at www.clemusart.com/explore/work.asp?accno=1133.1922. Give students these prompts:

1. The scene begins in the middle of some action. What are
    the central characters in the scene feeling and thinking?

2. Concentrate on the sounds in this scene. What sounds
    will you hear from the central action? What are the more
    general sounds that you will hear in this scene? To what
    can you compare these sounds?

3. How does this scene connect to the previous scenes and
    represent a *climax* for the plot?

4. Focus on characters in the crowd. Some are talking to each
    other. What are they saying to each other, and *how* are
    they saying it in these unusual circumstances?

5. What happens in the next scene to indicate the resolution
    or closure for all the conflicts? Who is involved? Where
    does the action take place? What, if anything, is said?

Stage 2. Connecting a Number of Images

It's easy to find provocative images. They appear in newspapers,
magazines, and books, and collections of photographs and paintings
are easily available on websites. One image might prompt a short
description or a whole story. Examining several images challenges
the writer to connect a series of events within a coherent narrative.
Give this latter challenge a context: an art curator needs to compose

the program for an exhibit of paintings by Edward Hopper and decides to connect several images to make one coherent story. (You can select images from another painter or illustrator if you wish.)

Give students the following task:

> Six paintings of artist Edward Hopper will be shown together at an upcoming retrospective of Hopper's work at the Chicago Art Institute. Dr. Amelia Cozzo, the exhibition curator, is composing the exhibit program and catalog. Dr. Cozzo believes that each of the six images can be appreciated not only on its own merits but also as a series of connected elements. Therefore, a two-page spread in the program will depict these six images, along with a story they suggest. She has hired you to write the story.

Here is a possible sequence of images, identified by title and the URL where you can find a depiction (you can substitute other paintings, prints, and drawings by Hopper or by another artist whose work holds the power to evoke stories):

> *Haskell's House*: www.nga.gov/fcgi-bin/tinfo_f?object=95419
>
> *Chop Suey*: www.ibiblio.org/wm/paint/auth/hopper/interior /hopper.chop-suey.jpg
>
> *New York Movie*: www.ibiblio.org/wm/paint/auth/hopper /interior/hopper.ny-movie.jpg
>
> *Room in New York*: www.artic.edu/aic/collections/exhibitions /hopper/artwork/193528
>
> *Office at Night*: www.ibiblio.org/wm/paint/auth/hopper /interior/hopper.office-night.jpg
>
> *Freight Cars*: www.artic.edu/aic/collections/exhibitions /hopper/artwork/193525

Students should follow this process:

1. Imagine that the paintings are windows through which you can view settings, characters, and actions, each one a scene from an ongoing story. Study each picture individually. In your notes, start jotting down

impressions. Who are the people? Where is the setting? When did the story take place? What is happening? How do the characters feel?

2. Draw conclusions about the *sequence* of the six images. How are they connected? How would one scene follow another to complete a story or to create a total effect?

3. The six images represent six frozen moments in a continuous narrative. What do you imagine has happened in the *intervening scenes*?

4. Focus on the *characters*. Who are they? Why are they in the place we see them? What feelings and motivations do they have? How are the characters connected to each other? What do the characters say to each other?

5. As you plan your story, imagine that your readers are not able to view the paintings. In your writing you won't refer to the paintings *as paintings*; rather, you'll provide all the images and descriptive details necessary to allow readers to picture each scene in their mind's eye. One way to create mental images is to compare the unfamiliar people, places, and actions in the paintings to other things readers might be familiar with.

6. What are your options for beginning the story? Do you want to begin with dialogue? Do you want to begin in the middle of the action? Do you want to begin with a substantial explanation of the background for the story?

7. Draft your story.

8. Show a completed draft to someone who *hasn't* seen the paintings. After this person has read your draft, show the pictures. Does your reader think your story portrays the images accurately? Is it a logical narrative representation of the sequence of pictures? Use the reader's comments to guide your revisions.

Stage 3. Fabricating a Feature Story

Writing a feature story helps students create *description, narration,* and *commentary.* They have to gather information and *incorporate quotes from interviews.* The composing process relies on *interaction with peers* at several stages, requiring attention to detail, imaginative invention, and oral rehearsal. (It also fosters an *empathic response to characters* similar to ones the writers might encounter in related literature. By adjusting the directions and choosing appropriate photos, you can use the activity to introduce a novel that depicts characters in a stressful situation, such as living in a time of war or political oppression.) To prepare, you need to gather the appropriate photos, assign students to groups, and be ready to model parts of the process (especially making decisions and solving problems when beginning the story and incorporating quotes from the interviews).

The photographs reproduced here (see Figure 4–1), taken by Depression-era photographers Dorothea Lange and Walker Evans, come from the Library of Congress' "American Memory: America from the Great Depression to WW II" collection. Library of Congress images are in the public domain and can be reproduced for instructional purposes. For additional photos, log on to http://memory .loc.gov/ammem/fsowhome.html.

EPISODE 3.1: **Set the scene for students.** What would it be like to have almost nothing at all—to be uprooted from your home and travel unfamiliar roads, with little money or provisions, looking for work? If you could meet and talk to the victims of economic ruin, what could they tell you about their life, their circumstances, their feelings, their dreams, and their hope for the future?

Give each group of four students a photograph that depicts the way many people lived during the Great Depression.

- *Tell them to examine the photograph carefully*: Describe the setting and character(s) in enough detail that someone not looking at the photograph will be able to picture the place, time, and person(s).

Figure 4–1. Images from the Great Depression

4–1a

4–1b

4–1c

4–1d

4–1e

4–1f

Photos (a–f), taken by Depression-era photographers Dorothea Lange and Walker Evans, are in the Library of Congress' *American Memory: America from the Great Depression to WW II* collection.

- Quickly jot down a list of words and phrases you think are likely to be in a description of the scene and the person. Working quickly, list words and phrases that would apply to the various senses: sight, feel, smell, sound, and taste. To what can you compare the sights, sounds, tastes, and feelings? What mood or prevailing feeling do these details suggest?

- Have students use their lists to answer the following questions:

    What is the physical setting?

    What can you see in the setting?

    What do the objects and structures in the scene look like?

    What does the person look like? Consider clothing, age, skin tone, hair, hygiene, emotional state, posture, gender, and size.

    What would it feel like to be in the scene? Consider the weather conditions and the relative comfort in the physical environment.

    To what can you compare the feeling of the scene?

    What sounds are you likely to hear in the scene?

    What do the sounds remind you of?

    What smells do you imagine are present in the scene?

    Can you associate any smells with the person(s) in the scene?

    Of what do the smells remind you?

    If you were a person in this scene, what tastes would you be experiencing? Remember that tastes are closely associated with smells, and that weather conditions and other environmental factors can affect taste.

    To what can you compare these tastes?

- Have students share their answers as a class. After listening to these descriptions, can students pick out the matching photograph? Whether they can or not will depend on how vividly and accurately students have captured the setting and characters.

- Ask students to write the description. Tell them to:

    Appeal to all the senses.

    Use *active verbs*, and avoid verbs like *is*, *are*, or *was*.

    Make *frequent comparisons* so that the connection to a more familiar image will allow the reader to imagine the scene and the character(s).

EPISODE 3.2: **Preparing for the interviews.** To collect information for their feature story, students must interview the person they have described.

- Have them prepare for the interview by writing a series of questions based on these considerations: *What is the focus or general goal of your story? What would you like to know about the person in the picture? What information do you need in order to support the substance of your story?* Tell them to anticipate possible answers so that they can prepare appropriate follow-up questions.

- Ask students, working independently, to write at least seven questions.

- Have students share their questions with the other members of their group and add effective questions suggested by others to their individual lists.

EPISODE 3.3: **Conducting the interviews.** In groups of four, have each student present his or her interview questions while the other group members play the character or characters and respond. Tell students to:

- Work slowly and carefully so that everyone has time to record the question and the character's response.

- Give the person being interviewed a name.

- Record the interview as a *transcript of a conversation*, like the script of a play.

- Record what the person says and how he or she says it.

- Capture any dialect or unique manner of speaking.

- Write the transcript in dark blue or black ink so it can be duplicated and shared.

EPISODE 3.4: **Sharing the interview data**. Form new groups composed of students who each have interviewed a different character. Everyone gets a copy of everyone else's interview. This means that the teacher will have to reproduce the sets of interviews for this stage in the process. Have each student read her or his interview aloud and explain what she or he learned about the character:

- What are the living conditions that the person now experiences?

- How does the person feel about his or her life at the moment?

- What hope does that person have for the future?

Ask students to read all the interviews silently to themselves and highlight portions that answer these questions.

EPISODE 3.5. Have students write their feature story. Tell them to:

- Begin with the description of the scene and a person in the scene.

- Rely on that person to tell his or her story.

- Incorporate material from other characters' interviews.

- Introduce each speaker so the reader can keep track of who is talking.

- Interrupt the speech of the characters from time to time to describe the movement, behavior, or emotional responses of the speaker.

EPISODE 3.6: **Editing and revising the draft**. Have students read their drafts carefully and check that they have:

- introduced the story with a vivid description of the setting and character(s)

- introduced speakers and quoted extensively from interviews to allow the speakers to tell their stories

- used quotations that provide insights into the lives of dispossessed persons

- punctuated all the quotes according to generally accepted conventions

Tell them they may also ask a classmate to check that their story is focused, accurate, thorough, and correct.

EPISODE 3.7: **Preparing the story for publication.** Tell students they are going to submit their story to a newspaper or magazine, so it needs to be error-free and neat: typed, double-spaced, one-inch margins. Tell them to use their word-processing program's spell-check feature, proofread carefully, and correct any errors. Have them print and hand in clean, edited copy. (An example of a student's work is shown in Figure 4–2.)

Figure 4–2. "A Day in the Life of the Dispossessed," by Laura Baumrucker

When my eyes met Sandy's eyes, they told me everything, trying to hide the pain her eyes enclosed. Her question remained the same. What is going to happen to us? Below her eyes you could see the immense need to sleep. Her eyes reveal great anxiety. Her true eye color fades more and more into a deep sorrow, pale and gray. She feels the same question: "What are we going to do?"

The winds carrying the dust throw open the worn tent. There is no way of stopping the wind, making it almost impossible to see. The stench of urine fills the little kids' clothes, worn, fading in color, not washed in months. It is very quiet at night, the silence filling the night skies, cool, with only the sound of the howl of an owl and the cry of the wolves.

Figure 4–2. "A Day in the Life of the Dispossessed," by Laura Baumrucker (*continued*)

"Before the Depression, I used to be a wealthy lady, along with my family. We had servants wait on us and did whatever we wanted; then suddenly from the day to night we were poor. This damn Depression hit and now we are here, from a big mansion to an old ragged tent. The hardest day I had to face was getting food for my children. The few things we had that were edible, my husband had given us before he passed away. You know he died from thirst, thirst of love, of patience, and of the courage to go on. He was a great man, such a hard working man, the man that was born in a rich golden crib and died in a cold foggy night there just on the floor or you might say in the dirt lying in his worn out clothes."

Mrs. Corona has three children. They all turn toward her, trying to conceal their faces against her clothes. The baby closes her eyes against the long wind blowing the sand in their faces, making it painful for them to even see, turning the world a dull brown. She stares at me and it remains quiet for awhile until she points out, "These men here, you see, provided me and my children with food and the safety of sleep; but it is still not the same without my husband. They help me get the food. I mostly stay here and cook it for them. That is the least thing I could do for their help."

One of the men at the migrant camp observed, "That's all you need to do to help around here. I mean, I see you and I feel for you and the three children. I feel bad and don't want them harmed. I mean, these people have nothing. I don't have much, but it's more compared to nothing, though it's really hard sometimes to get along. You lose your privacy. But still it's all we got for now. We have each other, today, tomorrow; and as

(*continues*)

Figure 4–2. "A Day in the Life of the Dispossessed," by Laura Baumrucker (*continued*)

long as we can, we have to stick together. I have no family with me right now. The only people now are somewhere else in the country. I just can't believe how our lives changed so much. I went from working making airplanes to working picking up crops in some old guy's farm to tending crops that are not even worth nothing now. I just hope that like this woman sitting right next to me, Sandy Corona, I have the will to keep going. If she can survive along with her three children then so could I."

You who have everything, you need to survive through this Depression, stretch your hand and help people like this poor woman with three little kids. Would you like to be in this position? Please help now, or help to lessen this pain for the people and the little kids.

EPISODE 3.8: **Reflecting.** Provide written feedback on students' feature stories. Also ask them to explain how they were able to complete their compositions successfully, reflect on what they learned by writing the story, and/or tell how they plan to develop their writing further. Have them respond to at least one of the following prompts:

1. Other students have told you they admire your work. Explain the process you followed to complete the story successfully.

2. A skeptical social studies teacher wonders whether you have learned anything about history or sociology by writing your story. Explain what you learned about people who lived during the Great Depression.

3. Respond to the questions and comments I've written in the margins of your paper.

5

What Makes This a Structured Process Approach?

As we hope we have demonstrated in this book, we believe that kids learn best when actively engaged in activities that interest them. This is the foundation of a structured process approach. Now that you have seen what teaching this way looks like, we'll lay out the basic principles that guided our planning and that might guide yours, too, going forward:

- The teacher usually identifies the task, such as writing a fictional narrative, although students may participate in deciding what they want to learn how to write. Even with the task identified, students often begin learning the processes through familiar activities such as writing a fable or a tall tale.

- Learning begins with *activity* rather than with the product of that learning. For example, the instruction in Chapter 1, rather than beginning with a story, begins with an activity in which students, in small groups, read a number of fables, discuss what they have in common, establish criteria for a well-written fable, and then write a fable themselves.

- The teacher designs and sequences activities that allow students to move through increasingly challenging problems of the same type. In the instruction in Chapter 1 students first learn how to write fables, then apply similar techniques while writing a tall tale. In Chapter 2, they write stories collaboratively.

- Students' learning is highly social, involving continual talk with one another as they learn procedures and strategies for particular kinds of writing. Throughout structured process instruction, students participate in whole-class and small-group discussions as they grapple with various problems and writing activities.

- The teacher designs the activities that take students through the particular writing process that produces the final product. However, in class, *the students are the ones talking and doing.* After helping the students identify the elements of a fictional narrative, the teacher has students apply these procedures to increasingly complex stories. The teacher's role is primarily to help students apply the strategies, not exercise a heavy hand in leading discussions and guiding the writing.

A structured process approach therefore places the teacher in the role of designer and orchestrator of student activity through which the *students themselves* make many of the decisions about how to write and how to assess the quality of their writing. Figure 5–1 is a more comprehensive list of principles that guide this approach. We and other teachers influenced by George Hillocks have outlined this approach in a number of publications, including Hillocks (1975, 2006, 2011); Hillocks, McCabe, and McCampbell (1971); Johannessen, Kahn, and Walter (1982); Johannessen, Kahn, and Walter (2009); Kahn, Walter, and Johannessen (1984); Lee (1993); McCann, Johannessen, Kahn, Smagorinsky, and Smith (2005); Smagorinsky (2008); and Smagorinsky, McCann, and Kern (1987). Several of these titles are available for free download at www.coe.uga.edu/~smago/Books/Free_Downloadable_Books.htm.

Figure 5–1. Principles of a Structured Process Approach

1. Instruction allows students to develop procedures for how to compose in relation to particular kinds of tasks. The processes that students use to write fictional narratives, for example, are different from those used to write essays that define.

2. Because different tasks require different procedures, writing instruction cannot rely solely on general strategies. Rather than simply learning "prewriting" as an all-purpose strategy, students learn how to prewrite in connection with a specific genre—fictional narratives, for example, in which case small groups of students might discuss a set of short narratives and identify criteria that distinguish a fable, a tall tale, or a recounting of a hero's journey.

3. With writing instruction focused on specific tasks, students work toward clear and specific goals with a particular community of readers in mind. For example, students might write a hero story that helps other students in their school contend with their real or imagined fears of facing down a bully.

4. Even with clear and specific goals, thinking and writing are open-ended. Individual fables, while incorporating the conventions of the genre, have varied characters, settings, events, and themes.

5. Composing is a highly social act rather than the work of an individual. Students discuss their compositions with peers at every stage of development. In a structured process approach, people learn to write by *talking* as well as by writing.

(continues)

Figure 5–1. Principles of a Structured Process Approach *(continued)*

6. The teacher identifies the criteria used to assess the writing. Students often help develop these evaluative criteria by discussing what they value in the writing they read. When the writing is tied to large-scale assessment, such as writing narratives for a district or state gateway exam, the criteria might already be in place.

7. The teacher *scaffolds* students' learning of procedures by designing activities and providing materials that the students may manipulate. Instruction begins with simple, manageable aspects. For example, instruction in how to write fictional narratives writing begins with activities in which students define the conventions of a particular genre by examining examples. Instruction then progresses through more challenging aspects of the writing, such as generating one's own ideas for characters, settings, and events. Attention to form comes later in the instruction when students have developed content to write about, rather than earlier, as is often the case with instruction in how to write the five-paragraph theme.

8. When possible, the teacher provides additional readerships for students' writing, such as having the students post their writing in the classroom or on a classroom wiki or submit their writing to a contest, the school newspaper, the school literary magazine, and so on.

Designing Structured Process Instruction

A structured process approach to teaching writing involves two key ideas: *environmental teaching* and *inquiry instruction* (Hillocks 1995).

Environmental Teaching

One important assumption that underlies environmental teaching is the belief that *each task we ask students to do involves unique ways of thinking.* By way of example, think of what is involved in three types of writing tasks: writing a fictional narrative about a leader, defining effective leadership, and comparing and contrasting two leaders. Each involves a consideration of leadership qualities, yet each relies on different ways of thinking and communicating one's thinking in writing. An environmental approach, then, stresses learning particular sets of *procedures* for engaging in specific sorts of *tasks*.

To help students learn to accomplish a new task, a teacher needs to involve students directly in developing strategies for undertaking that task. In other words, the teacher introduces activities that will help students learn *how* to do this new kind of thinking and writing.

A task in this sense involves both *doing* something and *thinking about how it's done* so that it can be done again with different materials. A task, then, may comprise writing a personal narrative, or comparing and contrasting similar yet different things, or arguing in favor of a solution, or defining a complex concept such as *progress* or *success*. Our goal for students is that when they complete this task, they are able to repeat the process more independently next time.

Inquiry Instruction

Inquiry is the particular structure through which students work, often in collaboration with one another.

Again, the teacher plays a strong role designing activities that provide the basis for students' inquiries into the problems they investigate. For fictional narratives, the problem may be how to generate criteria for and then create specific types of these narratives.

The students play with materials related to the questions they hope to settle through their writing. Play in this sense refers to experimenting with ideas. For example, students might examine a set of short narratives to determine how they are similar and judge what distinguishes a good narrative from a weak one. In small-group discussions, students bounce ideas off one another:

"All the stories involve animals as characters."

"Yeah, and the animals act like humans."

"They talk to each other. That's one way you know that they act like people."

"So the stories have to have dialogue."

Students' work is open-ended in that the activities may have a number of plausible solutions or outcomes. As the process advances, students explore possibilities for the substance of their stories, and match the substance to the criteria for defining the genre. Small-group discussions allow students to play with these ideas to try out solutions that may or may not ultimately figure into the final form that their work takes.

What Can You Expect When Teaching Writing with This Approach?

Preparing students to write well-developed, thoughtful fictional narratives is time-consuming. The detailed, systematic sequences in this book guide students through both thinking about and writing fictional narratives. The activities cannot attend to *all* the considerations in completing a task as complicated and interactive as writing. Realistically, before students are able to apply specific skills and strategies to new situations, they will need several experiences and appropriate feedback from you, from other students, and, if possible, from other readers. However, with continual reinforcement, the procedures that students generate should enable them to write strong narratives on future occasions when they choose or are called upon to create them.

Where Do You Go from Here?

This book and the others in this series provide specific plans you can adapt to your own teaching; they also introduce you to a process you can use to design original instruction based on your classroom and your students' needs. The guide below will help you design writing instruction using a structured process approach:

1. *Identify the task that will form the basis for your instruction.* Assuming that any general process such as "prewriting" differs depending on the demands of particular writing tasks, identify the task that will form the basis of the instruction. This task might be specified by a formal writing requirement and assessment provided by a mandate from the school, district, or state (e.g., argumentation); it might be writing that you believe is essential in your

students' education (e.g., writing research reports); it might be writing that students identify as something they want to learn how to do (e.g., writing college application essays); or it might come from some other source or inspiration.

2. *Conduct an inventory of students' present writing qualities and needs.* With the task identified, you will probably want to see what students' writing of this sort looks like prior to instruction. Doing so allows you to focus on students' needs and avoid teaching strategies they already know. You could take this inventory by providing a prompt like, *Write a narrative about a boy who stands up to a bully.* Then assess their abilities in relation to your *task analysis*, below.

3. *Conduct a task analysis.* Either by consulting existing sources or by going through the processes involved in carrying out the writing task yourself, identify what students need to know in order to write effectively according to the demands of readers. The task analysis should treat both *form* and *procedure.* The task analysis will also help you identify the evaluative criteria that you ultimately use to assess student work.

4. *Conduct an activity analysis.* Decide the types of activities that will engage students with materials that are likely to foster their understanding of the processes involved in the task. Identify familiar and accessible materials (e.g., fables and tall tales) for the early stages of their learning, and more complex materials (e.g., a hero's journey or a suspense story) for subsequent activities.

5. *Design and sequence students' learning experiences so that they provide a scaffold.* Design increasingly challenging tasks of the same sort using increasingly complex materials. Sequence these activities so that students are always reiterating the process but doing so in the face of greater challenges. The activities should present continual opportunities for students to talk with one another as they learn the processes involved in carrying out the task.

6. *Consider opportunities to teach language usage in the context of learning procedures for task-related writing.* Specific kinds of writing often benefit from particular language strategies. For example, fictional narratives are filled with descriptive words. Targeting language instruction to specific instances of its use helps overcome the problem inherent in discrete grammar instruction, which is that it fails to improve students' understanding of how to speak and write clearly.

7. *Relying on the task analysis, develop rubrics through which students clearly understand the expectations for their writing.* These rubrics may be developed in consultation with students, adopted from established criteria such as those provided for state writing tests or advanced placement exams, adopted from model rubrics available on the Internet, created by examining a set of student work that represents a range of performance, and so on.

8. *Provide many opportunities during the learning process for feedback and revision.* Students should be given many occasions to get feedback on drafts of their writing. This feedback can come by way of peer response groups, your written response to their writing, writing conferences with you, or other means of response.

A Structured Process Approach and Professional Learning Communities

Currently many school faculties constitute a professional learning community made up of collaborative teams. Structured process instruction is particularly effective in this context. Teachers together develop instruction and analyze student work. Teams use the student writing produced during the instructional sequence as a basis for discussing what worked, what students are struggling with, and what should be done differently or what needs to be added to the instruction. They collaboratively design rubrics for scoring student work so that expectations for students are consistent. Collecting data on student performance from pretest to final product allows the group to evaluate student growth, reflect on the strengths and weaknesses of the instruction, and plan future classroom activities.

Our own teaching has shown us that this approach can greatly improve students' writing. We look forward to hearing how you have adapted this approach to your own teaching and helped your students learn how to use written expression to meet their responsibilities as students, writers, friends, communicators, and citizens.

Questions for Reflection

1. What place does writing fictional narratives have in the middle school and high school curriculum?

2. Telling stories often relies on invention. To what extent is it possible to teach students how to invent the substance of their narratives?

3. Describe the process a writer would follow in producing a work of fiction. How is the process different from that of writing a persuasive letter or a research report?

4. Writing memorable fiction relies on the ability to make characters, settings, and action come alive. How can you help your students refine these skills?

5. What challenges might younger writers encounter with conventions and mechanics as they attempt to write a story? How can you teach the key concepts proactively?

6. It can be hard to agree what elements define good narrative writing, especially because many of the writers we admire break with convention. How can you help students define for themselves what distinguishes a well-written story?

7. How would you link writing fictional narratives with reading significant works of fiction? What are the advantages of doing so?

8. How can visual images or other appeals to the senses help students plan and produce fictional narratives?

References

Applebee, A. N., and J. A. Langer. 2009. "What Is Happening in the Teaching of Writing?" *English Journal* 98 (5): 18–28.

Bereiter, C., and M. Scardamalia. 1982. "From Conversation to Composition: The Role of Instruction in a Developmental Process." In *Advances in Instructional Psychology*, edited by R. Glaser, 1–64. Hillsdale, NJ: Erlbaum.

Blair, W. 1987. *Tall Tale America: A Legendary History of Our Humorous Heroes*. Chicago: University of Chicago Press.

Bruner, J. 1991. "The Narrative Construction of Reality." *Critical Inquiry* 18 (1) (Autumn): 1–21.

Frye, N. 1967. "The Argument of Comedy." In *Shakespeare: Modern Essays in Criticism*, edited by L. F. Dean. London: Oxford University Press.

Hillocks, G. 1975. *Observing and Writing*. Urbana, IL: National Council of Teachers of English.

———. 1986. *Research on Written Composition: New Directions for Teaching*. Urbana, IL: National Conference on Research in English and Educational Resources Information Center.

———. 2002. *The Testing Trap: How State Writing Assessments Control Learning*. New York: Teachers College Press.

———. 2006. *Narrative Writing: A New Model for Teaching*. Portsmouth, NH: Heinemann.

———. 2011. *Teaching Argument Writing, Grades 6–12: Supporting Claims with Relevant Evidence and Clear Reasoning*. Portsmouth, NH: Heinemann.

Hillocks, G., E. Kahn, and L. Johannessen. 1983. "Teaching Defining Strategies as a Mode of Inquiry." *Research in the Teaching of English* 17: 275–84.

Hillocks, G., B. McCabe, and J. McCampbell. 1971. *The Dynamics of English Instruction: Grades 7–12*. New York: Random House.

Johannessen, L., E. Kahn, and C. Walter. 1982. *Designing and Sequencing Pre-writing Activities*. Urbana, IL: National Council of Teachers of English.

————. 2009. *Writing About Literature*, 2nd ed., revised and updated. Urbana, IL: National Council of Teachers of English.

Kahn, E., C. Walter, and L. Johannessen. 1984. *Writing About Literature*. Urbana, IL: National Council of Teachers of English.

Lee, C. D. 1993. *Signifying as a Scaffold for Literary Interpretation: The Pedagogical Implications of an African American Discourse Genre*. Urbana, IL: National Council of Teachers of English.

McCann, T. M., L. Johannessen, E. Kahn, P. Smagorinsky, and M. W. Smith. 2005. *Reflective Teaching, Reflective Learning: How to Develop Critically Engaged Readers, Writers, and Speakers*. Portsmouth, NH: Heinemann.

Smagorinsky, P. 1991. "The Writer's Knowledge and the Writing Process: A Protocol Analysis." *Research in the Teaching of English* 25: 339–64.

————. 2008. *Teaching English by Design: How to Create and Carry Out Instructional Units*. Portsmouth, NH: Heinemann.

Smagorinsky, P., T. M. McCann, and S. Kern. 1987. *Explorations: Introductory Activities for Literature and Composition, 7–12*. Urbana, IL: National Council of Teachers of English.

Smith, M. W. 1989. "Teaching the Interpretation of Irony in Poetry." *Research in the Teaching of English* 23: 254–72.

Teaching Students to Write

The Dynamics of Writing Instruction series

- ▶ Argument
- ▶ Essays That Define
- ▶ Comparison/Contrast Essays
- ▶ Personal Narratives
- ▶ Research Reports
- ▶ Fictional Narratives

Designed to provide teachers with resources that ensure students gain the writing skills needed for success in college and careers

"These books will support teachers in their understanding of designing process-based instruction and give them both useful lesson plans and a process for designing instruction on their own that follows the design principles."

—Peter Smagorinsky, Larry Johannessen, Elizabeth Kahn, and Thomas McCann

Argument / Grades 6–12 / 978-0-325-03400-3 / 2011 / 96pp est. / $14.50
Essays That Define / Grades 6–12 / 978-0-325-03401-0 / 2011 / 96pp est. / $14.50
Comparison/Contrast Essays / Grades 6–12 / 978-0-325-03398-3 / Spring 2012 / 96pp est. / $14.50
Personal Narratives / Grades 6–12 / 978-0-325-03397-6 / Spring 2012 / 96pp est. / $14.50
Research Reports / Grades 6–12 / 978-0-325-03402-7 / Spring 2012 / 96pp est. / $14.50
Fictional Narratives / Grades 6–12 / 978-0-325-03399-0 / Spring 2012 / 96pp est. / $14.50

CALL **800.225.5800** WEB **Heinemann.com** FAX **877.231.6980**   DEDICATED TO TEACHERS